Leading Learners, Leading Schools

Leading Learners, Leading Schools is an exploration of the dynamics of schools as complex organizations. It presents a radical departure from established school improvement and effectiveness orthodoxies, offering a refreshing new approach to managing change and enhancing collective learning and creativity.

Based on the author's own experience of managing and leading schools, this book explores such questions as:

- How can schools learn as a generative process?
- How can schools become adaptive and co-evolve with their internal and external environments?
- How can education leaders 'navigate' their institutions out of the comfort zone and into the creative state?

The book concludes with a series of practical lessons for leading schools in complex conditions.

Leading Learners, Leading Schools will be of great value to reflective, action-oriented heads, principals and deputies, as well as academics and researchers in education management.

Robin Brooke-Smith is Principal of the University of Toronto Schools at the University of Toronto, Canada.

Leading Learners, Leading Schools

Robin Brooke-Smith

RoutledgeFalmer
Taylor & Francis Group

LONDON AND NEW YORK

First published 2003 by RoutledgeFalmer
11 New Fetter Lane, London EC4P 4EE

Simultaneously published in the USA and Canada
by RoutledgeFalmer
29 West 35th Street, New York, NY 10001

RoutledgeFalmer is an imprint of the Taylor & Francis Group

© 2003 Robin Brooke-Smith

Typeset in Sabon by BC Typesetting, Bristol
Printed and bound in Great Britain by
TJ International Ltd, Padstow, Cornwall

British Library Cataloguing in Publication Data
A catalogue record for this book is available from the British Library

Library of Congress Cataloging in Publication Data
Brooke-Smith, Robin.
    Leading learners, leading schools/Robin Brooke-Smith.
        p.   cm.
    Includes bibliographical references and index.
    ISBN 0–415–27498–2 (hard) – ISBN 0–415–274990–0 (pbk.)
    1. School management and organization. I. Title.

    LB2805.B82 2003
    371.2–dc21   2002033313

ISBN 0–415–27498–2 (hbk)
ISBN 0–415–27499–0 (pbk)

To Diane, James and Joe.
All part of the journey

Contents

Figures

Tables

Foreword

Michael Fullan

Complexity theory is forcefully making its way into organizational thinking and action. Robin Brooke-Smith's *Leading Learners, Leading Schools* is an especially powerful representation of this new genre because it is at once deeply theoretical and deeply practical. As principal of two unique and complex schools, Brooke-Smith is especially well positioned to grapple with the vicissitudes of the non-linear evolution of dynamic organizations operating in turbulent times.

The author first sets the stage by presenting the tale of the two schools in which he was – and, in the case of the second, still is – principal. It becomes immediately clear, as Brooke-Smith observes, that traditional approaches to studying school management are not up to the task. Even relatively recent approaches like 'school effectiveness and school improvement' err on the side of linearity. Rather, building on complexity theory, Brooke-Smith takes us on a more exciting and realistic journey. In his own words, he sets out to explore basic questions, such as: How can schools learn as a generative process? How can they become adaptive and co-evolve with their internal and external environments? How can educational leaders 'navigate' their institutions into what we will call the creative state (at the 'edge of chaos'), which is also the growing zone and is not always the 'comfort zone'?

Leading Learners, Leading Schools then proceeds to establish the theoretical case for a new paradigm: one that attempts to understand and guide dynamic systems by considering (1) rate of information flow, (2) connectivity, (3) variety and diversity, (4) power differentials, and (5) anxiety levels. He delves into the micro-politics or 'shadow systems' of schools. After revealing the shadow system, Brooke-Smith makes the case for the kind of deep learning that would be required to operate successfully in dynamically complex systems.

Finally, all of this is brought together in eight lessons for leading schools under non-linear conditions. These lessons are necessarily theoretically grounded and are not for those seeking an instant recipe for leadership. Brooke-Smith makes it clear that leadership for the future will require deeply reflective, action-oriented practitioners who are just as concerned about the conditions and processes of organizational learning as they are about periodic outcomes.

'Leading the intelligent school' in the twenty-first century demands sophisticated leaders who, as I said at the outset, are equally adept at thinking and action, and their dynamic connection. Robin Brooke-Smith makes a wonderful contribution to the small but growing list of books that do indeed attempt to go deeper (see also Fullan 2001, forthcoming, and Morrison 2002). Paradoxically, these books end up being also more practical because they map on to the complex reality of organizations in the twenty-first century.

Acknowledgements

I owe a considerable debt of gratitude to many people who have inspired me to write this book or who are a part of the story and journey that it contains.

My affection and deep respect go to many colleagues with whom I have worked over the years, especially at Shrewsbury School (UK), Edwardes College (Peshawar, Pakistan) and the University of Toronto Schools (Canada). I have learned most of what I know about schools and education from working with colleagues.

I would like especially to thank Professor Lynne Davies, Director of the Centre for International Education at the University of Birmingham (UK), for her unstinting support, advice, friendship and encouragement over several years. Also I owe thanks to Professor Michael Fullan, Dean of the Ontario Institute for Studies in Education at the University of Toronto (OISE/UT), for his encouragement and support.

My appreciation and thanks go also to Lt. Gen. (Rtd.) Muhammed Arif Bangash, Governor of the North West Frontier Province and chairman of the Edwardes College board of governors. His wise leadership and fine understanding of the nature of governance made him a rare and fine chairman. In similar vein I acknowledge the fine chairmanship of Bob Lord, Chairman of the Interim Board of Directors of the University of Toronto Schools. His humanity, acumen and wisdom have taught me a great deal.

Finally, and above all, I want to thank my wife, Diane, for putting up with more than she should have in far-flung places and for being a constant source of strength.

Figures 3.2 and 3.3 are reprinted with permission of the publisher. From *Complexity and Creativity in Organizations*. Copyright 1996 by Stacey, R.D. Berrett-Koehler Publishers Inc., San Francisco, CA. All rights reserved. www.bkconnection.com

Abbreviations

AKU	Aga Khan University
CAS	Complex Adaptive System
DDP	Departmental Development Plan
DFID	Department for International Development
DST	Dynamical Systems Theory
HOD	Head of Department
ICSEI	International Congress for School Effectiveness and Improvement
IGCSE	International General Certificate of Secondary Education
IQEA	Improving the Quality of Education for All
LEA	Local Education Authority (UK)
MIS	Management Information System
NWFP	North West Frontier Province
OISE/UT	Ontario Institute for Studies in Education at the University of Toronto
PD	Professional Development
R&D	Research and Development
SAT	Standard Attainment Test
SDIC	Sensitive Dependence on Initial Conditions
SE	School Effectiveness
SEI	School Effectiveness and Improvement
SI	School Improvement
SMT	Senior Management Team
ST	Senior Tutor
UFM	Unfair Means
UTS	University of Toronto Schools

Introduction

> Perhaps treating [schools] like machines keeps them from changing, or makes changing them much more difficult. We keep bringing in mechanics, when what we need are gardeners. We keep trying to drive change, when what we need to do is cultivate change.
>
> Peter Senge, in *Fast Company*, May 1999

Leading Learners, Leading Schools is addressed to all who have responsibility for – and an interest in – management, leadership and organizational learning in education, and indeed in any other human enterprise where deep learning and creativity are necessary. The title implies that leadership is as much about being prepared to learn as about being knowledgeable, and it is about encouraging others to learn in deeper ways where new, 'actionable' learning is developed. Anyone who has led a school or any kind of human organization or enterprise will know that this is far from simple.

When I was writing this book, I occasionally took time out to run with my dog, Jack, along the banks of the River Severn in my home town of Shrewsbury. Often my route would take me through an overgrown area known as Doctor's Field, which is overlooked by the house in which Charles Darwin lived as a boy. This is where Darwin loved to roam as a young man and where he learned his love for natural history. I would sometimes speculate, not too fancifully I think, that the massive task of exploring the inner workings or 'natural history' of modern organizations has some similarity to that other voyage of discovery by Darwin on the ship HMS Beagle in the early nineteenth century. The great task that lies ahead of understanding and unlocking human potential and creativity within organizations, and especially schools, is a matter of the utmost urgency to the development of the world in the twenty-first century. Furthermore, the implications for today's establishments – political, cultural and economic – may be just as profound as was the work of Darwin for the establishments of his day. The systematic study and practice of *management* is a very recent phenomenon dating from the early part of the twentieth century. It has coincided with the pioneering of the study of the human subconscious. Both sciences are in their infancy, and both need each other.

Leading Learners, Leading Schools was developed from my work as a school and college principal, a long teaching career in both maintained and independent schools in the UK, and within the context of links and research at the University of Birmingham and schools and colleges in that city. It charts new approaches and insights into the nature of modern schools and similar organizations, and it develops important new understandings for teachers, leaders, managers, policymakers and researchers. It will speak to you if, like me, you have been unhappy with the overall direction of the School Effectiveness and Improvement (SEI) movement, with its emphasis on factorial and simplistic approaches to improvement and change, or if you have a sense of frustration and anxiety at the increasing external demands being made by, and diminishing returns from, the dominant management imperatives of meeting 'outcome' and 'performance' targets by means of what I refer to as linear, mechanistic, old management-style methods. The reliance of so many policymakers, researchers and school leaders on the cosy lists of keys and factors to successful change propagated by so many in the SEI movement is, I would suggest, as valuable to them as the lamp-post is to the drunk – it gives more support than light.

What I have to say is stimulated by a sense of malaise in the education system (and other public services) and brings, I hope, fresh new approaches to the School Effectiveness and Improvement movement at the end of its nearly thirty-year development cycle. I have found that similar concerns are being expressed in many different countries around the world.

Significant numbers of senior and middle-level professionals have left and are leaving – retiring early, in many cases – in a state of disillusionment at a stage in their careers when they should be at the height of their effectiveness and personal and professional self-esteem. Others, who remain, complain of low morale and excessive bureaucracy. One may rightly ask, 'What is going on?' So much well-intentioned effort is evident. School Effectiveness and Improvement 'industries' have sprung up and flourished for decades giving rise to national curricula, local management of schools, 'opting out' of schools, parental choice, value-added approaches, league tables, assessment and examination reform, special measures for literacy and numeracy, OFSTED and so on.

This book is really about how we can recover the 'space' or conditions for organizational creativity and learning, which might perhaps lead to a return to the joy and thrill of being part of the world's greatest and most exciting enterprise – education. Our understanding of schools and similar organizations is at an exciting turning point. For too long the design of organizations has derived from traditional linear and mechanistic models. As we head into the fast-changing and challenging environments that undoubtedly lie ahead we will need radically different understandings, structures and processes capable of engendering deep creativity and 'double-loop' learning (see Chapter 3).

I outline important shifts in theoretical frameworks and practical applications in the management of quality and innovative schooling. The ideas I present concern what has become known as the 'learning organization' and relate to holistic management and the creation of organizational conditions congenial to *innovation, creativity* and *learning* at individual, group, institutional and system levels.

The ideas presented have been generated by practitioner observation and research in the workplace over a number of years and have led to a reappraisal of the theoretical frameworks underpinning the SEI movement and an exploration of what I have called Dynamical Systems Theory in relation to school management. I have not presented any ideas here that have not been a part of my own practice and reflection as a school and college principal, researcher and classroom practitioner. Indeed, even my varied experiences in managing a variety of other enterprises such as Himalayan mountaineering expeditions or educational aid programmes in Africa and Asia have informed my understanding of human groups and organizations and how they work and become deeply effective. Although the thrust is directed mainly at schools and colleges, much of the new approach outlined in the following pages has a wide application in organizations that are seeking to encourage high creativity and high levels of origination, ownership and energy among their members.

In addition to plentiful practical examples and insights, the book contains a good deal of quite complex theory. There is much in the saying, 'There is nothing so practical as a good theory.' I hope to demonstrate the truth of this in the chapters that follow. I have turned my back on the simplistic and reductionist approaches that have been so prevalent in recent decades and that have led to a succession of management fads and gurus. The real world of schools is complex, unpredictable, messy, and as a result full of fascination, heartache and wonderful possibilities as well as pitfalls. There are no quick fixes, as I shall attempt to show.

I believe that in any organization, and at all levels, there exists a well of creative ideas and the desire among individuals to make a difference and to be originators. At the same time there is all too often a level of obstructionism, opposition and even bloody-mindedness that cannot be ignored – though it is often bypassed in the literature. In the following pages I outline a powerful new approach that can unlock this creativity and transform our schools and other institutions. But it will first need a profound change of mindset. We have to get away from a things-strung-together linear approach – 'press this button, get this result' mentality. It also seems that much of the low morale alluded to above results from a failure to harness the basic creative urge that everyone brings to their work. If that creativity is not nurtured it can easily turn into negativity and obstructionism.

Rather than driving change and designing input-process-output systems in the pursuit of optimum outcomes, we will explore ways of cultivating organizational states that can lead to self-organizing creativity, deep double-loop learning (see Chapter 3) and unlimited innovation and origination. We will not lose sight of desired and mandated outcomes, but will give greater focus to institutional contexts that can engender transformations and creativity that can deliver outcomes beyond the dreams of current orthodox methods, mindsets and realities.

I owe a considerable debt to a number of major figures who have made a huge contribution to the study of complex human systems. Michael Fullan (1993, 1999) has been an inspiration as a colleague and friend and has almost single-handedly brought ideas of complexity and Dynamical Systems Theory into the mainstream of educational thinking. He has also brought the idea of moral purpose of teaching to centre stage, thus identifying the keys to motivating teachers as agents of change. Ralph Stacey's book *Complexity and Creativity in Organizations* (Stacey 1996) is a massive and important contribution to our theoretical understanding of organizations as complex adaptive systems. Chris Argyris (1999) has provided fascinating insights into ways in which organizations can be said to learn and the strategies – all too prevalent – by which individuals and groups resist deep learning. Lastly, and perhaps underpinning it all, is the pioneering work of Wilfred Bion (1991) of London's Tavistock Institute, itself built upon the work of the great psychologist Melanie Klein (1975). This work has opened up the psychodynamic elements of human interaction in organizations. I have attempted to interweave these strands of theory and, through empirical studies, have proposed a comprehensive set of working principles for managing schools in complex circumstances for deep organizational learning.

Lastly, it is important to emphasize that this book is but a small beginning. Ahead there lies a huge enterprise of researching and operationalizing the new dynamical systems approach. There is a widespread perception in the educational world that schools are on the verge of (indeed, in the midst of) a period of unprecedented change as the emerging information age presents unpredictable challenges and opportunities. What is less certain is the detail of what schools will look like in ten, twenty or fifty years' time. It can be argued that the basic structure and process of schooling has changed very little in the last hundred years. There is a sense that something profound is happening in society and that this change will inevitably have important effects on schools.

Since May 2001 I have been principal of the University of Toronto Schools (UTS): a high-quality 'laboratory school' part of whose mandate is to generate new knowledge and innovative curriculum and organizational best practice. As part of the Ontario Institute for Studies in Education (OISE) at the University of Toronto we have great opportunities to develop new models and ideas. We are seeking to contribute to this important exercise of crafting the institutions of the complexity age and to develop, research and implement new approaches to organizational learning in schools for the twenty-first century. It is the aim of UTS to play a significant role in helping to restore innovation and research to the hands of practitioners by crafting new models, methodologies and processes of research and development. The research community will need to develop a new research agenda to develop new management approaches deriving from Dynamical Systems Theory. We will need to generate knowledge and data from empirical studies and ethnographies to lend sharpness and focus to practice and to inform the training and education of leaders and managers at all levels. What I have attempted in *Leading Learners, Leading Schools* is to lay a foundation of understanding of a new approach to management for schools of the twenty-first century.

The structure of the book

Chapter 1 describes some empirical examples from my own recent experience that highlight the need for new approaches to and understandings of schools as living organizations (even organisms). I draw extensively on recent experience at UTS in Toronto, Canada and Edwardes College in Peshawar, Pakistan. Chapters 2 and 3 cover the essential elements of the new dynamical systems and complexity approaches to organizational theory and practice. It is likely that much of this may be new to readers. Chapter 2 sets the scene by placing the new theoretical base in its wider historical and cultural contexts. Chapter 3 explores the field of Dynamical Systems Theory in some depth in the context of a critique of the School Effectiveness and Improvement movement. The effect of this immersion in the exciting emerging fields of complexity and Dynamical Systems Theory will loosen some of the accepted perceptions and beliefs that are traditional and deeply ingrained in all our thinking about schools and human organizations in general. I cover new ground by using ideas derived from the theory of social autopoiesis. I explore ways of overcoming the (often dysfunctional) dichotomies between individual schools and their environments. This is important to school leaders and is also of special interest to policymakers and governments. In this chapter I attempt to find ways of overcoming the sense of 'being put upon' that has so plagued and frustrated the teaching profession.

Chapters 4 and 5 look at different aspects of the life and work of schools in the light of a dynamical systems approach. Chapter 4 explores the highly charged but rich vein of the micro-politics of schools and issues of governance in the search for new dimensions and new sources of creative energy. It is in the deep and often turbulent 'shadow system' of micro-political activity and what I have termed 'connectivity' that transformations are either made or broken. Chapter 5 deals with professional development and the search for deep learning and new behaviours (what is referred to as 'actionable' knowledge through double-loop learning).

Finally, in Chapter 6, I draw together the areas covered and draw up a set of practical lessons for school practitioners. Here I combine a summary of the theoretical learnings and a set of highly practical and useful guidelines for managers and leaders in their own practice.

This is not an attempt to create a new recipe for instant success for managers. No such thing exists in spite of the free flow of management fads and gurus and new approaches to school improvement in recent decades. I have attempted to break away from deeply ingrained ways of thinking about schools as organizations and to tease out ways of occupying that most elusive of localities – the creative state.

In order to gain a deep and lasting engagement with new approaches we might do well to heed the advice of the Swiss theologian Karl Barth: 'A good theologian does not live in a house of ideas, principles and methods, he walks right through all such buildings and always comes out in the fresh air again. He remains on the way.' This might make a good credo for educators in the twenty-first century.

A word of warning before we commence: many of the ideas that I present in this book will be less than effective without the presence of two basic conditions. First, a creative and dynamic school will require a sound and secure form of governance and clear forms of accountability at all levels. Second, the ideas presented will have difficulty in flourishing in the face of sustained and deliberately destructive and negative forces that can sometimes take hold of an institution. In such circumstances, more orthodox forms of management will be needed first to create a more normal situation before complexity and non-linear solutions can be instituted. The creative complexity that is explored in this book is a sensitive and delicate plant and will require firm guardians and well-grounded safeguards to allow it to flourish.

1   A tale of two schools

> The real trouble with this world of ours is not that it is an unreasonable world, nor even that it is a reasonable one. The commonest kind of trouble is that it is nearly reasonable, but not quite . . . It looks just a little more mathematical and regular than it is; its exactitude is obvious, but its inexactitude is hidden; its wildness lies in wait.
>
> G.K. Chesterton, *Orthodoxy*

I have been fortunate to hold the post of principal in two very interesting and very different educational institutions. I have also had the good fortune to have had a long and interesting career in a wide variety of schools, both public and independent, on four continents. In the process of grappling with the fascinating challenges of managing change in highly challenging circumstances, I quickly came to realize that the existing school management and improvement orthodoxies were quite inadequate to the task. The market is awash with management guides and manuals for the enlightenment of hard-pressed school principals and leaders. The single greatest weakness of these publications is the underlying assumption that change can be designed and delivered in a technocratic and predictable manner (what I have called below 'linear'). Would it were so simple. It is assumed that once success has been achieved in one institution it can easily be replicated elsewhere with only minor adjustments. Unfortunately the world of schools is not that simple; indeed, it is very complex, unpredictable and often chaotic. Any practising school head teacher or principal can attest to the extraordinary complexities, pressures and difficulties as well as the rewards and joys of the role.

One great question underlying modern organizational and management theory is 'What makes people and organizations *creative*?' In the past the questions have often centred on what makes organizations *productive* and how they can be controlled (managed) to deliver desired outcomes. Now we must go deeper than control and *productivity*. We have to look in radically new directions to tap the wellsprings of human and collective learning and creativity.

The heart of the process of managing change may lie in the processes of managing *anxiety*. Change can be very threatening. The unknown can be disconcerting. This concern for, and understanding of, *anxiety* – which is such a fundamental part of change – is almost completely absent from the orthodox literature about change in schools. There are many strategies used by individuals, groups and organizations to avoid or short-circuit change. We live in a time of unprecedented change; but, more important, we live in a time when change and the promotion of change have become a powerful new orthodoxy. There is no doubt that change is a ubiquitous fact and organizations that do not change often end in disaster. The ideas expressed and developed in this book are derived from a variety of experiences of the change process in schools on four continents. I have sought to create insights from a practitioner's viewpoint and to provide a theoretical framework developed in real practice in the real world. Too much educational writing derives from the sheltered academic world of education departments in the world's universities. Much of the material presented in this book has been cultivated and tested in the crucible of practice in the two very different institutions of which I have been principal. Examples and cases will be encountered as you read the chapters that follow.

The two schools that I will describe in this chapter are in many ways at opposite ends of the organizational spectrum in terms of their internal cultures and structures. They are in many respects as different as it is possible to get, and yet in both the problems and dynamics of change were remarkably similar. The first of the two institutions is Edwardes College, a prestigious institution in North West Pakistan for boys (and latterly some girls) aged from eleven to twenty-one. The second is the University of Toronto Schools (UTS), a multicultural, co-educational school for academically able students aged from eleven to eighteen attached to the Ontario Institute for Studies in Education at the University of Toronto (OISE/UT). UTS is a high-quality 'laboratory school' in partnership with OISE/UT. Perhaps the most obvious common denominator is the fact that both institutions were, in different ways, somehow inhibited in the processes of change and development. The reasons why each was 'stuck' were very different and very complex. In the case of Edwardes College, the organization was rigid, hierarchical and deferential in the setting of a highly conservative Islamic culture. Few staff members felt empowered to take responsibility. In the case of UTS, almost the opposite was true. It had a well established culture of 'academic collegiality' and there was a tradition of open debate and lengthy discussions on a wide range of topics. The school had a very flat organizational structure with very little in the way of traditional middle-management; for example, there were no heads of department. UTS was situated in a secular western city and university with a progressive and liberal culture. Thus, in the two very different cases, the change process was inhibited.

Edwardes College is a rare institution that has served the educational needs of the North West Frontier Province (NWFP) for a century. It straddles the secondary–tertiary divide with nearly 1,500 students aged from sixteen to twenty-one. There is also a school section, Edwardes College School, occupying a portion of the same campus, which caters for about 160 pupils aged eleven to sixteen, providing qualifications up to local 'matric' and overseas IGCSE. It is an old missionary foundation that during its hundred-year existence has achieved a pre-eminent position in the North West Frontier Province and has the highest reputation throughout the country.

The college was stable, but in many respects – especially in teaching, learning and management – deviated from 'good practice' as delineated in much of the recent School Effectiveness and Improvement literature. In spite of this situation, there was a complacent rhetoric of the college being 'the best', a 'fine institution', 'the best in the Frontier', with 'wonderful traditions' and so on.

Edwardes College had little if any sense of dynamic forward direction, few specific educational values other than preparation for exams. There were features of the institutional and educational culture that would act as obstacles to change. These included:

1   A tendency to autocratic centralism with high power differentials. This was a strong feature of the culture of the region.
2   A highly deferential approach to authority within a steeply and rigidly stratified hierarchy. Again, this was a feature of the local culture.
3   A reluctance on the part of many staff to shoulder responsibility and carry out delegated functions and tasks. Correspondingly there was a tendency to shuffle responsibilities up the line to the person at the top. Closely connected to this was a deep fear of making mistakes and, therefore, of holding responsibility – 'in case it goes wrong'.
4   An antiquated administrative system based on a highly labour-intensive team of clerical staff working with slow and inefficient procedures inherited from a bygone age. The principal and 'administration' were expected to make all the decisions with few obvious forums for consultation.
5   Ambiguous and problematic forms of governance.

The University of Toronto Schools (UTS) by contrast has some very different features. Whereas at Edwardes College I found I had to spend much time lowering power differentials and empowering staff by delegating authority, at UTS I found a situation where power differentials were very low indeed and a very flat organizational structure had developed, leading to an active micro-political culture. There was nothing deferential about life at UTS.

UTS is a remarkable – perhaps unique – institution that has developed certain dynamics and customs that constitute a well-defined and distinctive school culture. This is both a strength and, in some contexts, a limitation. The key aspects of the school culture are:

1   A very participative and involved student body of exceptional ability selected through a series of highly competitive examinations, and a very active parents' association.
2   A very supportive and involved alumni association of great distinction. (In recent years the school has produced nineteen Rhodes scholars and two Nobel laureates.)
3   A highly 'democratic' process of staff involvement in policy formation and decision-making leading to what many saw as a rather convoluted process of consultation.
4   Before 1993 the school was fully funded by the Ontario Government. The withdrawal of this funding in 1993 proved to be a crisis and at the same time a liberation and spur to growth and development. UTS is now fully fee-paying but has not arrived at a settled sense of its true locus and identity in the educational world of Ontario and the University of Toronto. A sign of the intent of the UTS community has been the tremendous achievement of a campaign known as the 'preserving the opportunity' fund to provide a substantial bursary fund to ensure that no student who gains admission to the school will be turned away for lack of financial resources.
5   A fixed point in the UTS universe has always been the University of Toronto and OISE/UT. This provides the potential for wonderful resources, partnerships and dimensions to the work of the school. It has perhaps been one of the school's most under-exploited aspects.

UTS is mandated to model an original and powerful practitioner-based innovative Research and Development (R&D) capability. It also has a mission as a centre for teaching practice for pre-service trainee teachers. Building on its unique partnership with OISE/UT it is working to develop cutting-edge methodologies and expertise in practitioner innovation and creativity capable of wide international significance in the coming decades. In this way UTS can play a significant role in helping to restore innovation and research to the hands of practitioners by crafting new models, methodologies and processes of research and development.

Both these institutions occupy rather unorthodox and anomalous places in the educational world leading perhaps to more opportunities for innovation than is possible for schools in the mainstream. Each had a degree of autonomy that allowed it the space to experiment. Neither was embedded in a wider public bureaucracy, though each was attached to a greater or lesser extent to a university. Both presented very clear contexts in which I found that orthodox management understandings were inadequate for the deep change and transformation that were needed. The traditional linear mechanistic approaches were inadequate and failed to explain the realities in which I found myself.

The management structure at Edwardes College was one of dizzying verticality with, in effect, the principal at the top with a largely titular vice-principal and the rest of the staff arrayed in their time-honoured and time-sequenced hierarchy of seniority. It was a caricature of the old 'command and control' hierarchical model. In this situation the system control parameter (see Chapter 3) of *power differentials* was high, with the effect of holding the organization in a rigid, frozen state.

The immediate practical result of this was that the principal was potentially an all-powerful autocrat in a largely disempowered system where deference to the 'boss' was everything and deference by the junior (in age and service) to the senior (in age and service) a powerful norm. Although the principal had all the appearance of power, in reality he was also very disempowered by the system; in fact, the whole system was disempowered. By contrast, at UTS everyone appeared to be empowered by the dominant culture of scholarly collegiality; but in reality the system was disempowered.

Early on at Edwardes College I found that my day was largely consumed by decision-making and dealing with matters great and small – mainly small. As nobody seemed capable of taking (or, more to the point, willing to take) decisions, everything had to come to the principal for written approval – right down to the purchase of small amounts of stationery. Soon I was so busy and bogged down with minutiae that there was no way I could possibly be involved in anything of strategic or operational importance. My diary for 14 January 1996 reflects this problem:

> It is becoming clear that one big problem here is delegation. Nobody seems to want to bear any responsibility. All sorts of petty matters come to me for a signature and for my decision. It is hard to see how this is to be broken down. I have the feeling that if I do succeed in delegating, there are such powerful political currents running among the staff that delegated powers would be misused or abused in one way or another. . . . An anonymous letter came today making all sorts of allegations about various members of staff. (Anonymous letters were a common occurrence throughout, and my policy was officially to ignore and file anything that was not signed.)

This situation allowed the staff to continue to operate in ways that were pretty ineffective without the risk of uncomfortable and unwanted intrusion from 'above'.

The matter of gathering information and taking action on aspects of student performance, pastoral matters, discipline and so on was equally frustrating and difficult. In a body of 1,500 students there was virtually no machinery or structure dedicated to pastoral or academic management of students and their routine progress.

Clearly there was a need for new structures. The emergence of structures had been inhibited by the existence of a steeply hierarchical system that had progressively disempowered many staff. It seemed obvious that before new strategic intents could be articulated, future goals set and 'forward' motion started, there must be restructuring. There is much in the literature that suggests that building a shared vision in conditions of complexity comes later (Fullan 1993, 1999, Stacey 1991, 2001, 2002, Beer, Eisenstadt and Spector 1990). In the words of Fullan (1993: 28):

> Visions are necessary for success but few concepts are as misunderstood and misapplied in the change process. . . . Visions coming later does not mean that they are not worked on. Just the opposite. They are pursued more authentically while avoiding premature formalization.

At an early staff meeting I presented the idea of a ship putting to sea and the need for it to be seaworthy with a working engine and efficient crew and so on before setting course for any long-distance destination. This was rather colourful, perhaps banal, imagery, but it made the message clear.

There was a bewildering array of very difficult and sensitive challenges and problems that could easily have got out of hand. There were instances of missing files and a chaotic filing system. The college financial system was in great need of thorough reform, and a team of clerks carried out routine bookkeeping and the management of the accounts working by hand with a series of old-fashioned ledgers and accounting systems. We moved rapidly to computerize all the accounting systems – a bold leap into the modern world. Most alarming of all, each student's fees were paid in monthly in cash by the individual concerned at a window in the college office. This of course brought serious attendant risks as it meant large amounts of cash were held there. All salaries were also paid out in cash from the office, adding to the difficulties. Each month on pay day huge sums had to be brought in from a bank in the city.

In order to improve this situation I ordered an inquiry into the workings of the fee and salary payment systems and requested recommendations on alternative methods of managing the money for fees and salaries.

The situation highlighted the dangers inherent in handling many millions of rupees in cash. The inquiry found that making these payments through a local bank was quite feasible, so I immediately set in train the process of bringing this situation to an end by arranging this. The processes involved in this change provide a very interesting microcosm of the change process as outlined in Table 1.1.

Table 1.1 Stages in problem-solving

Stage 1	Challenge/problem	Problem identified
Stage 2	Innovation suggested to prevent repeat crisis and improve efficiency	New payments and banking arrangement suggested
Stage 3	Consultation and discussion	Problems, obstacles and practicalities considered collectively
Stage 4	Finalization of innovation or plan	Written, detailed plan prepared
Stage 5	Implementation	Innovation implemented for trial period
Stage 6	Feedback and monitoring	Teething troubles and malfunctions observed, recorded and discussed
Stage 7	Amendment and fine-tuning	Continual checking for performance

In this change and innovation we followed a type of action research or feedback cycle. As illustrated in Table 1.1, we identified a problem, devised a solution/innovation, consulted and planned to get the best possible plan, implemented the plan, monitored the operation, reviewed progress through feedback, revised and fine-tuned the operation.

What we did was really nothing more than applied common sense. We were in fact acting like a complex adaptive system (see Chapter 3). We reacted to our internal and external environments to create effective change that enabled us to navigate more effectively in our specific 'landscape' (Roos 1997, Merry 1995, Stacey 2001, 2002).

Consultations (Stage 3) were limited to clerical staff who handled the college finances as well as the bursar, vice-principal and one or two senior academic staff. The senior staff murmured about possible difficulties, but I went ahead all the same purely in the interest of removing vast amounts of cash from the office along with the attendant dangers.

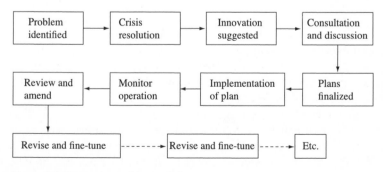

Figure 1.1 Stages in problem-solving

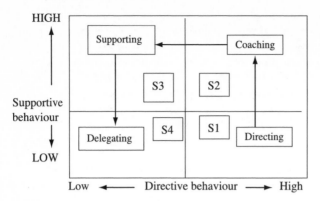

Figure 1.2 Stages in group development and leadership style

Source: adapted from Blanchard (1994)

In terms of situational leadership (Blanchard 1994, 2001) it is helpful to chart the state of maturity of the team. Fig. 1.2 depicts the stages through which teams or groups pass as they mature and achieve degrees of competence. This theoretical framework for considering situational leadership has proved useful as a guide to our practice and is helpful in analysing our work. The group directly involved in planning, implementing and monitoring the change can be described as being in group development Stage 1 (S1) in Fig. 1.2.

In this stage, directive behaviour by leaders is appropriate. In a crisis situation it was necessary to be very task-oriented. We had vast amounts of cash awash in the office.

We monitored the new procedures for several months and gradually they became the accepted norm. This, then, can be called an S1 (group development Stage 1) episode. A national bank was appointed to open a small booth on the campus. All students now collected their fee slips in triplicate and took them to the bank booth just two hundred metres away. There they deposited their fees, leaving one slip with the bank, one with the college office and keeping one for themselves. As the new procedures became established, the staff involved moved swiftly through the group development stages from S2 (coaching), S3 (supporting) and S4 (delegating). (See Fig. 1.2.) As soon as everyone involved understood the workings of the new system very little further coaching or supporting was required and the processes became embedded and automatic.

There were many other challenges at this stage. There were staffing problems which, although fairly routine, required input from a variety of academic staff some of whom had their own very distinct and sometimes idiosyncratic agendas. There were localized jealousies between individuals.

There were huge – almost intolerable – pressures at admission time in August from families and friends of hopefuls who had not made the entrance grade. Sometimes these pressures were of a political nature. These and many other human and organizational complexities had to be confronted in the context of a college that was a Christian foundation in a conservative Islamic context (around 20 per cent of staff and 5 per cent of students were Christian, with the remainder Muslim). The college was normally an exemplar of inter-faith harmony. Nevertheless there were naturally, from time to time, some underlying tensions that came to the surface.

If one adds the multitude of other difficult interactions, problems and issues that washed over and around the college one gets a flavour of the unpredictable, confusing, complex and perplexing reality of this large institution. Much of the school improvement and management literature fails to take into account the sorts of messy complexities which these examples illustrate.

Identifying areas in need of change

There is no rule book on how to act in such situations. Each situation demands its own response, style and approach requiring certain characteristics and competencies. The most important of these may be adaptivity, sensitivity and intuition. Daniel Goleman *et al.* (2002) in their book *The New Leaders* identify six main leadership styles as key elements in the repertoire of an effective leader who is capable of exercising 'emotional intelligence'. Effective leaders need to adapt their style to fit the circumstances (Gunter 2001).

Complex phenomena are composed of simple constituents. Effective function derives from the complexity of structures and interactions that bind the simple building blocks together. Dysfunction at Edwardes College was evident. I surmised that the communications and interconnections (information and connectivity control parameters – see Chapter 3) were ineffective. The institutional 'neurons' (to use a biological metaphor) were not firing properly. We needed to look at the way the pieces were put together. In my description above of developments at the college I have placed certain areas, practices and structures under the spotlight. In so doing I was investigating the connections and informational structures that lead to the emergence of the qualities of sustainable effectiveness for our environments. In doing this I have sought to identify types of informational exchange, types of connections and modes of interaction that most predispose the institution to learning and effectiveness. This process of close scrutiny is intended to help find the self-organizing mechanisms and principles underlying a complex adaptive system.

The examples above provide some interesting insights into the basic structures and principles of organizational development.

- Human groups and organizations are constantly changing and moving through a cyclical process of development and/or recession. Change is inescapable; but directed, purposeful change requires inputs, context and controls.
- Organizations change and adapt constantly in response to changes in their internal and external environments.

Purposeful and effective organizations not only change and adapt as in the second statement above, but through a process of information-gathering, processing and recycling are able to change proactively so that they positively affect their internal and external environments. In effect they learn how to anticipate the future and choose their own futures out of a vast array of possibilities. This is done by developing flexible internal structures that have an enhanced capacity to process and act upon information.

One might at this stage hypothesize four zones of decision-making:

1   Central decisions
2   Local or delegated decisions
3   Consultation: central and peripheral
4   Influencing.

Most important decisions are taken centrally, but consultation processes occur to varying degrees and at varying levels. Unnecessary over-consultation can be counterproductive and can lead to wasted staff time. Under-consultation can lead to a sense of disempowerment and remoteness from the decision-making processes. Consultation is usually focused on the concerned groups and individuals. After necessary discussion, decisions are taken and where possible key staff should be integrally involved in the final decision process and the widest possible agreement reached. Sometimes there may be a number of possible courses of action open to the group. Often there may not be much choice between them. All the options should be discussed and understood, and the one chosen should be accepted and owned by all. Thereafter the process of constant review and monitoring will proceed. It is at this cutting edge of decision-making that the processes of Complex Adaptive Systems (CAS) are most potent and most obvious by their presence or absence.

At UTS, decision-making had been considerably circumscribed by a process of over-consultation through an extensive use of committees without an effective reporting procedure and line of accountability. There had been consultation without effective context or structure. Indeed, the culture was one of 'academic collegiality' with an assumption that all decisions would be taken by an open vote of all the staff.

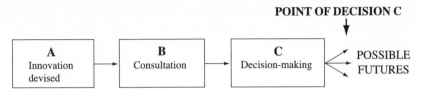

Figure 1.3 Point of decision

At point C in Fig. 1.3 there is sometimes a clear and obvious line to take, but more often there are several competing alternatives. Much may hang upon making the right choice at this point. The decision made will often lead to a chain reaction of future developments and here the key principle of chaos theory, 'Sensitive Dependence on Initial Conditions' (SDIC), comes into play. The difference between decisions X and Y can be the difference between chaos on one hand and orderly, creative progress on the other. It is, therefore, to these key points and processes of decision-making that our close attention should be directed. It is here that the institution must above all display its intelligence. It is at the point of decision that learning is at its greatest. It is here that powerful feedback, information-gathering, interaction and effective discourse can give the institution powerful and dynamic advantages.

One must of course face the possibility of radical and profound disagreement. What if the principal and vice-principal disagree even after detailed consultation? What if there is division among staff members? The answer is in two parts. First, continue with the discussion and brainstorm the problem. Look outside the institution if necessary to bring in more information to bear upon the situation. If all else fails, then of course it is the principal's role to exercise the casting vote or to defer the decision until greater clarity and agreement are achieved. However, the very richness of the information flow, the flexibility of the decision-making process and the culture of consultation should make profound disagreements over policy and decision-making a much less likely occurrence. Traditional 'command and control' modes of management with high levels of power differentials are more likely to breed misunderstanding and disagreement due to their restricted communication system.

Complex Adaptive Systems (CAS) should engender a culture where healthy and constructive disagreement is encouraged. Indeed, the clash of ideas is the very life breath of a dynamical system. It is at these slightly disturbing 'points of decision' that the system enters the zone of disequilibrium; it moves towards chaos in the sense that a wide variety of future possibilities open up. Some of them may be chaotic in their eventual outcomes, some may lead to frozen outcomes and some may lead towards creative disequilibrium.

The efforts to create working structures described in this chapter were guided increasingly by the insights of the science of complexity and dynamical systems theory and the need to maximize information and learning in the interests of seeking out and actualizing creative future courses of action.

The need for new approaches to school management

The main focus of *Leading Learners, Leading Schools* is centred upon innovation and change theory in the context of school improvement. This has been modified in the light of dynamical systems theory and group psychodynamics. This in turn has led to a major critique of the School Effectiveness and Improvement (SEI) framework and methodology as operating in an outdated linear mechanistic mode (Chapter 3). In its place I have proposed and espoused in my practice a non-linear, complexity model which accepts the deep unpredictability of the details of change. I have sought to describe, in our practice at Edwardes College and the University of Toronto Schools and elsewhere, processes and understandings that can lead to deep double-loop organizational (and individual) learning by occupying what we have called the space for creativity or the learning zone (Chapter 3). In the process of implementing change agendas, I have borne in mind a number of theoretical formulations around the processes of innovation. These theoretical studies include the broad-based work on the management of change that embraces the 'rational' and 'political' as the two great strategies of innovation. 'Rational' is characterized by the RD&D (research, development and diffusion) approach. 'Political' approaches involve competing rationalities such as the opposing forces for and against change. This theoretical base is explored in the context of the change agendas at the University of Toronto Schools and Edwardes College.

Important developments have occurred in this field in recent years, so much so that researchers are beginning to talk of a 'paradigm shift' (Fitz-Gibbon 1996). This thinking has its origins in the scientific exploration of complexity and chaos theory (e.g. P.C.W. Davies 1987, 1999, Waldrop 1992, Johnson 2001, Holland 2002, Kauffman 2000).

In the context of school improvement, the new insights suggest that schools are complex systems and will manifest 'discontinuities, catastrophes, unevenness and unpredictability' (Fitz-Gibbon 1996) like any other similar complex system. Fitz-Gibbon charts the evolution of models of change and research in schools as follows:

The effectiveness focus   Here, research concentrates on the 'correlates of effectiveness' which generate 'factors' that claim to lead to school improvement. The results, however, have often been too generalized and anodyne, leaving the question 'how' largely unanswered.

The improvement focus Here, research concentrates on collecting empirical evidence of school improvement efforts with the expectation that, if repeated many times, it will yield a picture of reliable and workable school improvement measures and policies.

The complexity or feedback focus With the rise of complexity and chaos theory, the idea of arriving at replicable 'nomothetic' laws is increasingly questioned, and it is here that a sea change may be occurring. The complexity model focuses on accurate and quality feedback, which is becoming increasingly available through computer-controlled information available at all levels in the system.

The whole validity of strategic planning is increasingly questioned under conditions of rapidly changing unstable environments where Sensitive Dependence on Initial Conditions (SDIC) makes detailed outcomes unpredictable (Stacey 1996, 2001, 2002, Wheatley 1999, 2002). My central and guiding theme is that school improvement and effectiveness have been propagated through an inappropriate dominant management framework that is not effective in complex environments. SEI needs to be liberated and enriched within a new dominant paradigm supplied by dynamical systems theory and complexity and chaos theory. Complexity has become an important field and has played an important part in my thinking on the management of change at Edwardes College, UTS and elsewhere. This is so much so that the following two chapters develop the concepts and principles of complex dynamical systems in the context of education.

Practitioner research and development

An important element of schools in the twenty-first century will be their capacity to carry out practitioner research, development and dissemination. Schools will be a major locus of research activity using action research and other well-developed practitioner research methodologies. UTS has a mandate to pursue practitioner research in the context of the laboratory school.

In the process of managing change at UTS and Edwardes College, theory and practice have been in cyclical dialogue, questioning and testing each other, and as a result new theoretical and methodological insights emerged and were themselves tested. The data and narratives of everyday practice were set against theoretical frameworks. In a sense the central cyclical feedback process of complex dynamical systems is incorporated into daily life of professional educators.

My thinking was informed by the management ideas and theory presented in the SEI literature, and over time my approach has changed and evolved to encompass ideas from Dynamical Systems Theory (Stacey 2001, 2002, Mitter 2001) and related fields. This was the result of simultaneously

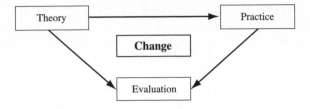

Figure 1.4 Cycle of action research for deep learning

learning, researching and operating as lead practitioner where I grappled with the complex realities of the everyday life of schools. I have taken change as a baseline and sought to build around it an iterative process of deep learning as depicted in Figs 1.4 and 1.5.

The cyclical iterative process depicted in Fig. 1.4 has a striking similarity to the way in which agents in a complex dynamical system behave, using a cycle of *discover, choose, act* to inform behaviour and to modify or preserve existing schemas (see Chapter 3).

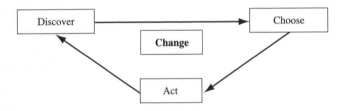

Figure 1.5 Cycle of system cognition

In describing and surveying the actual process and struggle for change I have sought to identify in the midst of the untidy, sometimes acrimonious, often confusing, frequently warm and amusing and always and essentially complex, the outline patterns in the 'chaos attractor' (described more fully below) and to reach for the essential control parameters that determine the state of the system. (Five are described in Chapter 3.) The control parameters, *rate of information flow, connectivity, diversity, power differentials, and anxiety,* are all related to what Fullan (1999: 13) describes as, 'the quality of relationships among organizational members'. It became clear to me, in my practice in the very different organizational cultures described above, that 'collaborative culture' depended upon these control parameters.

In spite of identifying these five control parameters it is important to emphasize that change and learning are still not simple or unproblematic. There is no magic bullet that can deliver creativity and learning. There can be no definitive theory of change precisely because change is complex and non-linear. Fullan (1999: 21) acknowledges that it is

> A theoretical impossibility to generate a theory that applies to all situations. Definitive theories of change are unknowable because they do not and cannot exist. Theories of change can guide thinking and action . . . but the reality of complexity tells us that each situation will have degrees of uniqueness in its history and makeup, which will cause unpredictable differences to emerge. . . . It is the task of change theorists and practitioners to accumulate their wisdom and experience about how the change process works.

2   Old paradigm, new paradigm

We must have a little chaos in us to give birth to a dancing star.

Friedrich Nietzsche

This book is about educational management and leadership for knowledge creation and learning in educational institutions. Fullan (1999: 15) emphasizes the centrality of 'knowledge creation' in institutions: 'We cannot understand and attempt to harness change forces until we also find a way to increase the capacity to incorporate new ideas.'

In this chapter I will give an overview and flavour of the new approaches of complexity and chaos theory that are moving rapidly beyond traditional linear, mechanistic approaches. I will set this new complexity approach within the wider sweep of changes in scientific thinking from the eighteenth-century scientific and industrial revolutions to developments of more recent times. In Chapter 3 I will explore these new approaches in more detail so that we can develop a set of principles to guide the actions of school leaders seeking to enhance organizational learning.

Recent developments – especially in the last twenty years – in scientific thinking are emphasizing order and pattern, change and creativity in complex dynamical systems in an attempt to understand the key processes of 'self-organization' and 'emergence' as two features of complex systems. Chaos and complexity theory derive originally from the physical and biological sciences. Although such approaches have become common in the business world, educational research and practice have been slow to realize the full implications of this new approach for schools. In this chapter I will explore the theoretical bases of possible new approaches to education emerging from what has become known as 'complexity' or 'chaos theory' (e.g. P.C.W. Davies 1987, 1989, Gleick 1988, Nicolis and Prigogine 1989, Prigogine 1980, Lorenz 1995, Ruelle 1993, Kaufmann 1993, Morrison 2002, Holland 2002, Johnson 2001).

Complexity is a young science which is feeling its way cautiously – and sometimes not so cautiously – towards some potentially very exciting new avenues of research and practice. However, some circumspection is needed when assessing certain ideas to emerge from this new approach, particularly when looking at human organizations. I will therefore make a tentative, critical and cautious exploration of its central theses.

I will explore some basic questions. How can schools learn as a generative process? How can they become adaptive and co-evolve with their internal and external environments? How can educational leaders 'navigate' their institutions into what we will call the creative state (at the 'edge of chaos'), which is also the growing zone and is not always a 'comfort zone'?

We will explore the importance of 'far from equilibrium' states in what theorists are calling the 'poised organization' and the creative possibilities that emerge in the 'phase transition' zone, which is rather alarmingly referred to as the 'edge of chaos'.

The mechanical, reductionist scientific world view appears to be undergoing rapid and radical change. In its place there is emerging a new set of understandings in which interconnectedness, information, learning and adaptivity are becoming the priorities. An important symptom of the times is the fact that wealth is now increasingly defined in terms of information rather than material and energy which dominated former periods: 'The real and controlling resource and the absolutely decisive "factor of production" is now neither capital nor labour. It is knowledge' (Drucker 1993).

Throughout history the richest people in the world have been those who controlled and owned the most valuable commodities. In the past these commodities have been elements such as land, machinery, oil or gold. Now the richest man, Bill Gates, owns very little of material substance but controls and owns the gateways to information and 'connectivity' and likewise his company Microsoft is the richest corporation on earth. Information is king, and there is talk of a weightless economy. The new realities of the information age demand that we understand and adapt to the new realities.

In the midst of such sweeping changes, it is likely that the schools of the twenty-first century will be barely recognizable in terms of the structures and models we have been used to. Tim Brighouse (chief education officer of Birmingham, UK) captures the exciting possibilities for schools in the future in a lecture given in London in October 2000:

> It is, for example, especially difficult in the infancy of our helter-skelter electronic age to decide what our schooling system will be like at the heart of the twenty-first century. Yet in that very description lie the seeds of some of its distinctive features. It is, and will remain for some time, the age of creative technological change, which will affect the habits of humankind and their institutions. So teachers will have to be people who see change as an inevitable part of their life: indeed as leaders of change. It will be their voice, which increasingly dominates the discourse of the time. Moreover, in a way quite different from the past, teachers will not be seen as learn*ed* but as *learners*.

> (My italics)

Brighouse goes on to develop a vision of schools as 'communities of learners' in a connected world where distance no longer has any meaning. The vision can include e-tutoring, classrooms without walls using the Internet and intranets and video conferencing, and schools gathering together in connected 'collegiate academies'.

A central question is, therefore, what is inhibiting organizations from continuously adapting to their environments? Interest in the field of 'change management' has grown dramatically among business academics and the corporate world. As yet continuous adaptation by institutions is not a fully understood management concept. What theorists increasingly agree upon is that an institution's ability to create 'organizational knowledge' is crucial. The educational world has lagged behind the corporate world in the field of Dynamical Systems Theory (DST). Very little serious research or study has been devoted to its application to school management. Many of the reforms and initiatives that have cascaded into schools in the United Kingdom and elsewhere have often appeared to have a less than optimum or sometimes a negative impact. There is, as yet, a limited understanding of the self-organizing adaptability required by complex adaptive dynamical systems. What appears to be lacking is an effective set of operational theories that are in tune with the nature and complexities of schools in the information age. My present purpose is to develop such a set of theories and to ground them in management practice.

The field of complexity suggests that the most complex dynamical systems can display a breathtakingly patterned, purposeful and apparently simple mode of operation. Through a process of self-organization there can emerge a beautiful and patterned simplicity and coherence of form and function out of the most complex of systems. Take any natural self-organizing and adaptive entity and you will find that an astonishing depth of complexity of process and structure enables the beauty and ease of function. Examples are numerous and include animal forms, weather systems, the human brain and social systems.

Some important general questions underlie our investigation.

- In what sense can we talk about organizational learning? How do organizations learn and generate 'actionable' institutional knowledge? What are the mechanisms and operational theories that can help us understand 'system cognition' or learning?
- In what ways can we explain the interplay between individuals and higher levels of 'social aggregation' that can be said to constitute organizational learning?
- How do you create information-rich schools and school systems capable of deep and collaborative learning modes?
- What are the best ways of reaching deeply into the inner resources of the school and at the same time reaching out to rich veins of outside support and knowledge?

- How do you create space, structures and dynamics that allow for 'emergence'[1] and institutional learning (Nonaka and Nishiguchi 2001)?
- How do you actively capitalize on and develop the understanding that the whole is more – far more – than the sum of the parts? Can we legitimately think of schools as groups of individuals where those groups are real entities and irreducible to the individuals that constitute them? In what sense should we attribute to such groups capacities for thinking, enquiring, and learning?
- What implications do the findings of complex dynamical systems have for student learning, the curriculum, structures and pedagogy?

So we will be making an inquiry into new ways of thinking about schools as human organizations. This has important implications for organizational design and management practices in many if not all types of institution.

Theory is important, and before we can begin to design new ways of structuring and organizing the educational process we must have a theory that matches the changing times.

The so-called complexity paradigm has so far not penetrated very deeply into the field of educational management and organization. There have been only limited attempts to operationalize these concepts (Richards 1990, Parker and Stacey 1994, Drazin and Sandelands 1993, Sterman 1989, Senge 1990, 2000, Stacey 1996, 2001, 2002). The knowledge diffusion process may first require that the basic concepts be introduced to a new audience in an accessible language, followed by their use metaphorically. Maybe at that stage there can be an attempt to operationalize the concepts for mapping the theoretical framework and for further empirical testing.

The 'Machine Age'

Now, at the end of the scientific, industrial 'Machine Age', the old smoke-stack industries no longer dominate the leading economies. Many accepted certainties of the old scientific modes of understanding are increasingly challenged or superseded by new insights and approaches that are being opened up by the power of the computer. It is easy to forget how recent is the rise of the universal personal computer.

Mechanical and linear modes of understanding are giving way to more organic metaphors. Schools and educational systems have often been slow to change and adapt to new realities. Adaptivity is a central process of development, and central to adaptivity are feedback and information. This means that my focus will be heavily upon the quality of feedback, information systems and knowledge creation as crucial processes in institutional effectiveness. Furthermore, it becomes clear that an understanding of mechanisms of collective learning is likely to become central to concepts of institutional development which in turn will accelerate the transformation of the school as we have known it into a much more responsive and adaptive reality.

The modern world remains deeply influenced by a scientific paradigm originating from the pioneering of physical science, mechanics and engineering in the industrial and scientific revolutions of the eighteenth and nineteenth centuries. The 'Newtonian' scientific world view conceived of the universe in terms of a great machine and posed mechanical laws associated with a mechanistic world. This view of the universe as essentially predictable, uniform and mechanical permeated not only the sciences but also politics, business, economics, education and virtually all social institutions.

In all spheres of life it was believed that stability, equilibrium, order and predictability could be achieved if the laws of science and society were applied consistently and accurately. This was a world dominated by linear modes of calculation and explanation. In constitutional matters 'checks and balances' were spoken of. 'Fine-tuning', 'rates of return', 'oiling the wheels', and other mechanical metaphors were and are widespread as means of explaining reality in institutions. France under Napoleon boasted an educational system in which the central ministry of education could tell you at any time of the school day exactly what page of which textbook every child of a given age was studying – predictability perfected.

In the nineteenth century, education systems were developed in Britain, Prussia, France and the USA which were to a large degree modelled upon and influenced by the industrial and scientific worlds in which they arose. Schools and universities run by religious orders and denominations gradually gave way to national secular systems of schooling. By the end of the nineteenth century these new secular systems were focusing increasingly upon scientific and technical knowledge. This pattern was replicated in the countries of South America, Africa and Asia. Today, mainstream educational systems around the world possess a high degree of structural and pedagogical uniformity, as is shown by the existence of formal school sites and buildings, certificated teachers, standard textbooks, curricula based upon a map of learning divided into specific discrete subjects and mass examinations. A great deal of the science and maths curriculum is devoted to pre-twentieth century concepts and topics with the quantum sciences and complexity theory poorly represented.

It is easy to forget how recent these mass educational systems are. One must realize that they may be temporary features of our lives.

> We are so accustomed to education systems as permanent features of our society that it takes an effort to remember that they have been (and may remain) a very temporary constellation. They have been with us a shorter time than Coca-Cola (invented in 1857), and may indeed be a 'hiccup in history'.
>
> (Davies 2000: 73)

The emerging sciences of complexity help us to see educational systems and processes in a new light and to see them as co-evolving with their environments.

So far the new thinking has hardly touched schools and educational systems. The mechanical, linear, predictable and equilibrium systems of the industrial, scientific era are slowly giving way to more organic, non-linear, unpredictable and complex adaptive systems. Brighouse takes a realistic view about the pace of change in schools and teaching: 'The character of the twenty-first century profession will become clearly distinctive not in the first ten years but nearer the mid-point.'

The 'Newtonian–Cartesian' scientific paradigm

From the early eighteenth century, industrialization and the rise of scientific technology became a powerful driving force in history. With the rise of modern capitalism and the industrial age, the technological scientific system came to dominate the world and effectively created a new civilization. Underlying this tremendous historical change was a profound change in human ways of knowing and understanding. The Newtonian positivist world view came to permeate every human enterprise. Newton's physical laws, Galileo's cosmology, Euclid's geometry combined in simplicity and power to give an immensely potent and influential basis for scientific understanding as well as providing an underlying influence on social, political, educational and economic thinking. The Newtonian model co-evolved with the emerging industrial societies. Newtonian ways of thinking spilled over into every other discipline and area of life.

While Newton presented fundamental laws to explain and manipulate physical reality, philosophers, social reformers, politicians, educators and economists sought out basic principles and laws that governed the proper functioning of society and social phenomena. The central assumptions of the Newtonian–Cartesian positivist world view may be characterized as follows:

- Reality is absolute, immutable and certain with a high degree of predictability.
- Reality observes, abides by and is explained by a few basic laws.
- Where there is ambiguity or unpredictability this is a sign of lack of information, inaccurate calculation or insufficiently developed theory.
- Reality can be explained within a unitary and simple space–time continuum.
- Reality is concrete and substantial; made up of matter.
- Propositions are either true or false. There is little if any room for ambiguity, paradox or unpredictability.
- Reality is best understood as a hierarchy from atoms to living organisms through the vast variety of life to the higher primates. This is reflected in a similar ordering of human societies.

- Reality is composed of separate, discrete, interchangeable parts that relate to one another in essentially mechanistic, linear and predictable ways.

From these essential understandings of reality came the belief that mankind stands outside and above the physical reality. Human consciousness had the capacity to comprehend and control the natural and physical world objectively. Nature was seen as other and separate and capable of complete explanation, measurement and subjugation by the application of rational thought.

New paradigms

Many of these ideas and attitudes have now been superseded or vastly altered by the emergence of new developments in scientific thinking such as evolution, thermodynamics, electromagnetism, relativity, quantum physics, psychology and the new sciences of chaos and complexity. Nineteenth-century developments in the fields of evolutionary theory forced scientists to think of the world as less a machine and more an emerging, growing, evolving and ever-changing system in which structures of ever-increasing complexity developed from building blocks consisting of much simpler forms.

In spite of these changes, the old thought patterns continued to dominate public policy as well as the shape and structures of institutions. This was reinforced by the rapid growth of secular educational systems where positivist thinking continued to dominate at first in Europe and the United States and later in the colonial world. Darwin's theory of evolution was slow to be included in school curricula and even today causes much controversy in schools in the USA where it is under attack from religious conservatives.

It is no longer possible to cling to notions of a world that is essentially simple and predictable. The new sciences are opening up immense new vistas for understanding the workings of reality in all its complexity and unpredictability. In 1942, J. Jeans in *Physics and Philosophy* was able to say: 'Today there is a wide measure of agreement . . . that the stream of knowledge is heading towards a non-mechanical reality; the universe begins to look more like a great thought than a great machine.'

There is an increasing awareness of the fact that we are an integral part of the reality we observe. It is no longer possible to take an aloof and totally objective stance in the face of the world. The new realities leave us with a sense of wonder in the face of a magnificent, mysterious and living cosmos. We belong to that cosmos and are integrally part of it. Quantum Physics and Relativity have removed the firm foundation from beneath the classical scientific world view. Quantum Theory asserts that reality is not built upon a firm and immutable material base. Reality is better understood in terms of the dance of primary particles, which can be conceived of as either particle or wave (the wave-particle duality of light).

Again, it is clear that these powerful ideas have had minimal impact upon the way society and educational systems are organized. The structures and assumptions underlying the design and operation of schools remain to a large degree rooted in the logic and language of the industrial scientific age. This worked in the industrial era, but is likely to be increasingly dysfunctional in the information age. It is perhaps hard for us to realize how deeply this thinking has permeated everything about our corporate and institutional world.

Chaos and Complexity Theory

Chaos and Complexity Theory have developed rapidly in the latter part of the twentieth century, enhanced and enabled by the computing and simulation capacities of modern computers. In my experience of grappling with all the factorial models of school effectiveness and school improvement, I have increasingly found the limitations of traditional 'reductionist' models (Brooke-Smith 1999). The very point of such models in schools is to reduce to simplicities the complexities of organizational life, giving a focus on unitary dimensions such as 'high expectations' or 'home–school links' or 'safe and orderly environment'. Nothing is simple in the day-to-day culture of schools, and such simplicities did not fit the slippery and messy realities I found myself confronted with. The insights of complexity and complex adaptive systems have provided a powerful set of theories to help explain and manage the realities I was engaged in.

In the new paradigm there is a realization that schools and school systems, like most other human organizations, may be so complex that they are inherently unpredictable and their realm of developmental possibilities is so vast as to be incalculable. This is an important realization for practitioners, researchers and policymakers and requires a new mindset for our approaches to change. The new approach of chaos and complexity is beginning to grapple with this realization. Complex systems, like schools and colleges, are non-linear and dynamic, with a great number of independent variables or agents interacting with each other in a great many ways. They are, therefore, messy and complex. They do not necessarily correspond with the pure elegant solutions of traditional scientific approaches. Such complex systems need to balance order with disorder, stability with change. This balance point has been termed the 'edge of chaos', where a system is balanced between stability and turbulence. This point 'at the edge of chaos' or controlled disequilibrium is where a rich diversity of interactions can occur between a host of interdependent variables which brings about the 'miracle' of 'self-organization' and 'emergence'; and these are the hallmarks of complex systems.

Another hallmark of complex systems is their 'adaptive' nature and capacities. Complex systems, unlike mechanical linear ones, are not passive but respond to and interact with their surroundings and environment for advantageous change. The key mechanism for this adaptive and interactive process is 'feedback'. An obvious example of such an adaptive non-linear feedback mechanism is the human brain, which constantly organizes and reorganizes billions of neural connections and pathways in order to learn profitably from complex and sometimes confusing experiences.

Feedback systems in schools are a key mechanism that can operate on the interface between stability and turbulence to produce creative adaptive complexity. This, therefore, leads to a tentative model for a new generation of research and practice that takes as its focus feedback systems. In this 'complexity model' feedback becomes an important tuning instrument by which the subtle balance between order and chaos, stasis and motion can be achieved and modulated and by which the system is propelled to what is known as 'emergence'.

From this complexity model it becomes clear that the number of effective connections and the quality of the communication in a system are key variables. Who is talking to whom, about what? Where is information flowing? How reliable, accurate and relevant is the information? How is information stored, used, made available and archived or destroyed when no longer of value? How is information ordered, reordered, set into hierarchies and used to construct internal models that enable the institution to act and adapt effectively in its environments? It is clear that institutional learning is aided by maximizing accurate and valid feedback and, naturally, minimizing inaccurate, false, misleading or irrelevant feedback.

Naturally, there are important issues here concerning the social constructions of relevance, accuracy and meaning in these feedback loops. We need to ask how decisions are made concerning the use or redundancy of information. There is a difference between information pure and simple and the more subtle forms of knowledge, meanings and competencies that the institution can and must generate. Nonaka and Tacheuchi (1995) state that the success of Japanese companies lay primarily in their skill and expertise at 'organizational knowledge creation' and they developed ideas about *tacit* and *explicit* knowledge. Fullan (1999: 16) dwells at length on these ideas.

> In brief, the secret to success of living companies, complex adaptive systems, learning communities or whatever terms we wish to use, is that they consist of intricate, embedded interaction inside and outside the organization which *converts tacit knowledge to explicit knowledge on an ongoing basis*.
>
> This is a fantastic insight into how learning takes place in collaborative cultures, and into why formal planning fails. Formal planning is logical and analytical and introduces explicit knowledge, not bad

in itself but woefully inadequate. Organizations good at conversion tap into the values, meanings, day-to-day skills, knowledge and experiences of all members of the organization (including the outside-the-organization connection) and make them available for organizational problem solving. . . . Isolated cultures have no means of getting at these sources of knowledge and no means of mobilizing the competencies and motivation of organizational members.

The process of knowledge creation is no easy task. First, tacit knowledge by definition is hard to get at. Second, it must sort out and yield quality ideas; not all tacit knowledge is useful. Third, quality ideas must be retained, shared and used throughout the organization.

(Author's italics)

The important point here is the vital distinction between *tacit* and *explicit* knowledge within the institution.

Complex adaptive systems

This new complexity approach has been greatly assisted by the power of modern computers, which have for the first time put within our grasp the ability to model and simulate the vast quantum of data needed to understand dynamic complexities. In the old paradigm what cannot be properly or easily measured and what is 'extraneous' is discounted so the scientist is left with a soluble equation, proof or result. Likewise some educational research has minimized the complex human factors involved in school systems, which are made up of imperfect people with ambitions, follies, politics, and 'all the ills that flesh is heir to'. The same has been true of neoclassical economics where what is described does not always match the chaotic and unpredictable realities of real economic situations (Waldrop 1992).

Within a school context there are many obvious and formal feedback systems, but many more informal feedback loops at individual, interpersonal and subgroup levels. Such systems seem to share three vital characteristics.

First, such a system comprises a network of 'agents' acting together. These 'agents' may be the atoms in a molecule, cells or neurons in a brain, firms in an economy and so on. The key feature of the way these agents operate is that they occupy an environment produced by their own interactions with each other within the system. In the school or college context, this means that agents such as individual staff, students, departments and stakeholders will be constantly interacting to produce their environment. The quality of the interaction and interchange is, therefore, a key variable, and much of the quality of this interaction depends upon feedback. It is also important to note that the control of complex adaptive systems is frequently very dispersed and decentralized. Brains have no master neuron and economies have a frustrating tendency to defy attempts at centralized control; the literature tends to confirm that human organizations are more efficient if power and control are dispersed throughout the system.

The second important feature of complex adaptive systems is that they have many levels of organization, with agents at one level serving as building blocks or constituents of a higher level. In this way a group of individuals compose a department and a group of departments a faculty or division right up to the institutional or corporate level. The important point in this connection is that, in effective adaptive systems, internal structures (i.e. agents) and their behavioural schemas (see Chapter 3) are constantly undergoing rearrangement and revision in the light of the learning and experience they gain through feedback. Just as a human brain learns through experience and knowledge by rearranging billions of neural networks so a firm or school will from time to time re-pattern its agents and modify its behaviours and structures to gain more efficiency in the pursuit of its goals. In other words, complex adaptive systems have a high capacity to learn, evolve and develop.

The third characteristic of these systems is that they develop the capacity to adapt nimbly in anticipation of, or response to, changes in the environment. A school system may anticipate changes in the prevailing economy and diversify its curriculum to prepare students for new kinds of work, or it may provide programmes to counteract perceived future changes in social conditions. A school or school system, therefore, often depends upon its ability to recognize external and internal changes and adapt swiftly and accurately in response. Complex adaptive systems are constantly making predictions based on their various internal models of the world and the environment in which they operate; in other words they make a series of implicit assumptions about 'the way things are out there'. It is, however, important to recognize also that these internal models are not just passive, immobile blueprints, but they are active. They can come to life a bit like a computer program sub-routine and 'execute' in order to produce behaviour in the system. They are like the building blocks of behaviour and can be altered, rearranged and tested as the system learns and gains experience through its feedback loops.

Another model that may be of help in understanding the dynamics of change in complex systems is one based upon the concept of 'mutation'. A great deal of complexity research indicates that a system can exhibit complex and lifelike behaviour only if it has the right balance of stability and fluidity (Chapter 3). To imagine how this operates in real human organizations one can take the example of a school or business corporation. The school may be stable and mature, with highly traditional leaders and deeply conservative stakeholders. All the agents have become well adapted to each other. There is little pressure for systemic change or development. However, the agents cannot forever remain static because of the slow drip of time, and eventually one or more agents may experience a 'mutation'.

Let us suppose that a principal retires and a new person brings in a cascade of new ideas, people and practices. A firm may be in the same static condition, but here there is a major technological breakthrough that leads to a huge pressure on it to change or die. What we have in both cases is a sudden breakdown of the previous equilibrium that threatens turbulence or chaos, but which, if well managed, can lead to creative complexity on the 'edge of chaos'.

Powerful principles of dynamic and effective management of schools and school systems will emerge as we explore how to move systems constantly towards and into this zone of transition where stability and fluidity blend to provide a creative milieu for exploring new possibilities. Understanding the detailed mechanisms of these processes is the area that researchers should increasingly be drawn into.

One of the great modern pioneers of chaos and complexity, Illya Prigogine, a Nobel prize-winning physicist, confronted head-on the great unanswered contradiction at the heart of modern science. On the one hand, the famous second law of thermodynamics holds that everything in the universe is heading towards entropy: the great clock of creation is running down, and after a great number of eons all the energy in the universe will be dissipated into a uniform, undifferentiated mass of inert matter. On the other hand, the Theory of Evolution describes how, at least in part of the universe, the movement is towards increasing order, complexity, sophistication, energy and structure.

> While some parts of the universe may operate like machines, these are closed systems, and closed systems form only a small part of the physical universe. Most phenomena of interest to us are, in fact, open systems, exchanging energy or matter with their environment.
>
> (Prigogine 1980)

Clearly, schools are open systems and, along with most other social organizations, attempts to treat them purely in the old mechanistic terms are unlikely to meet with much success. Margaret Wheatley (1992) describes the new imperatives of the information age in the corporate world thus:

> Look at almost any organization in America that is based on some strong assumption of the world as a machine. In a machine you have separate parts. They have to be well tooled; they're replaceable. You cannot tolerate change with a machine; you want a stable environment. That mentality led us to create organizations based upon what I would call seventeenth-century assumptions about the world as a machine. What we are seeing today is the death of seventeenth-century models. . . . In the future information will be the load-bearing structure of organizations. It won't be architecture. It won't be organizational charts. It will be – What are your information networks? How extensive are they?

Who do they bring in? And we are looking to a future, whether we like it or not, in which we will not be shored up by rigid structures, because rigid structures do not work.

As yet we seem to know very little about communication and the transmission of information and knowledge in complex adaptive systems. We are beginning to learn that systems that are far from equilibrium can produce new structures and characteristics through a spontaneous process of 'self-organization':

> Survival has to do with gathering information about the environment and responding appropriately . . . bacteria do that, by responding to the presence or absence of certain chemicals and by moving. Trees communicate chemically too. Computation is a fundamental property of complex adaptive systems. . . . Any complex adaptive system can compute; that is the key point. You don't have to have a brain to process information in the way I'm talking about it.
>
> (Lewin 1993: 138)

We are beginning to realize that no matter how much we know about meteorology, for example, and no matter how powerful our computers may be, detailed and specific long-range prediction is not really possible. We can know a lot, but we cannot predict. We can know with some certainty that it will be warmer in the summer months, but we can know almost nothing about the likelihood of rain or wind next week. So complex systems are radically unpredictable in detail but they exhibit clear overall patterns of behaviour. In terms of organizations this means that they must be sufficiently flexible to adapt. It is hard to influence and intend specific changes in detail. They must be able to learn, and this involves being responsive and creative, which in turn rests upon the ability of the organization to acquire, transmit and process information both internally and externally.

Stocktaking

Before moving on it may be helpful to attempt a few basic statements of progress so far. I am suggesting the idea of the arrival of a new era. Once major new technologies take hold – especially ICT – then societies change forever. The invention of the printing press in the fifteenth century is an example of an immensely powerful cause of change in history. It was the early-modern-period equivalent of the Internet. The changes in scientific thinking outlined above have co-evolved with an explosion of information:

- Structures of social organization have so far altered relatively little in the same time.

- Changes that are taking place are focused upon the generation and use of information.
- The times ahead will demand new ways of thinking, new and more effective theory, new modes of organizational learning and adaptation which will produce institutional structures, systems and processes that themselves have the generative and dynamic capacities for further adaptation built into them.
- The Newtonian–Cartesian 'Machine Age' paradigm is rapidly giving way to new modes of understanding.

In this book I have fashioned a set of operational principles and practices for use in schools (and similar institutions) for sustainable and adaptive effectiveness and tested them against experience of change management in schools and colleges. I have sought to draw up some essential design principles for structures, processes and information handling in schools. We now move on to a detailed study of the new thinking.

The key lessons for schools will relate to the following central concerns for schools in the twenty-first century (Table 2.1). These areas will be the

Table 2.1 Nine key lessons of the dynamical systems approach to schools

---

1   Strategic planning is problematic and often counterproductive. (Strategic planning allows little space for self-organization and the unexpected.)

---

2   Vision and mission cannot be mandated or imposed. (Complex systems have 'fractal' echoing structures and discourses that support shared vision.)

---

3   Feedback: self-amplifying and self-regulating are essential for deep creativity. (Virtuous circles lead us to new ground; monitoring keeps us on track.)

---

4   Interpersonal interactions can mean that one plus one equal far more than two. (A central theme of complex systems is the power of what happens in the spaces and relations in-between.)

---

5   Emotional atmosphere and geography of schools are crucial to success. Anxiety levels are the key parameter. (There is no deep learning without anxiety: we must simultaneously cause and contain anxiety.)

---

6   Modulation of five system control parameters can lead to double-loop learning. (The management of context is central to the new management.)

---

7   A school's environments is really a part of itself. (Schools and their environments must come to a new understanding of each other.)

---

8   Great leverage is achieved by using the principle of Sensitive Dependence on Initial Conditions (SDIC).

---

9   Creating and living with paradox is the secret of all life and learning.

---

focus of the present book, and I will draw out some detailed lessons under each heading. They are a supplement to the wonderfully creative eight basic lessons presented by Fullan in *Change Forces* and *Change Forces: The Sequel* (1993, 1999).

Fullan underpins all his understandings of effective change with the notion of moral purpose. All that I have to say in this book takes that as an essential given. Without sincere and shared moral purpose very little is possible in schools.

Note

1 In the study of complex systems, the idea of emergence is used to indicate the arising of patterns, structures or properties that are not sufficiently explained by reference to the system's pre-existing components and their interaction. The concept of 'emergence' becomes especially important when a system displays the following characteristics: a) The overall organization of the system appears to be more salient and of a different kind than the components. b) When the components can be replaced without decommissioning the whole system. c) When the new global patterns or properties are radically novel with respect to pre-existing components.

Issues involved in using emergence as an explanatory construct include: how causality is to be understood in such systems and what general laws or principles can be discerned in the emergent patterns, structures and properties.

3 Dynamical Systems Theory

A new approach to school improvement

> It is this silent swerving from accuracy by an inch that is the uncanny element in everything. It seems a sort of secret treason in the universe.
>
> G.K. Chesterton, *Orthodoxy*

I make no apologies for embarking on a lengthy exploration of new theoretical bases for the management and leadership of schools. First, it is of immense importance for teachers, leaders and managers to gain a firm grasp of the new directions in which organizational theory is moving. Second, the world is changing so fast that new frames and understandings of organizations are urgently needed. In the following chapters I will root the theory in practical cases and experiences.

I have stated above that my concern for and interest in developing a new working framework emerged as a result of my experiences as a school and college principal. The various lessons and findings of school effectiveness and improvement provided the initial focus and framework for my thinking on the improvement programme at Edwardes College. We aimed to take the best practice and principles from current School Effectiveness and Improvement (SEI) sources and apply them with cultural sensitivity. My purpose in this chapter is to review the research, theory and practice of School Effectiveness and Improvement and to indicate its limitations for sustainable improvement. I also question the fundamental framework underlying SEI as incomplete and unsuitable in today's rapidly changing environments and suggest that a dynamical systems framework – as yet largely missing from SEI research and practice – is more appropriate.

I rapidly came to the conclusion that much of the existing and very large corpus of research findings and exhortation in the field of SEI lacked a crucial dimension, which we may provisionally call 'dynamic'. SEI seemed to a great extent to be confined and inhibited by being grounded in a faulty or at least inadequate management paradigm based upon a limited understanding of how organizations work on the basis of dynamically structured *relations*. The real issues facing us were: how to energize the institution, how to cultivate change and how to nurture the *relations* needed for institutional learning for sustainable fitness. As time went on I discovered that this involves understanding the relationships that constitute the system and the circular processes of system 'cognition', 'feedback' and 'self-making' or autopoiesis.

SEI has been operating comfortably within the confines of a theoretical framework in which the primary mode of explication is analysis. Thus systems are annihilated in the process of trying to understand them. The all-important *relations* are lost because they are not amenable to categorization. Stafford Beer (Maturana and Varela 1980) captures the impact of this world view in a devastating passage on the modern university.

> It is an iron maiden, in whose secure embrace scholarship is trapped. For many, this is an entirely satisfactory situation, just because the embrace is secure. A man [sic] who can lay claim to knowledge about some categorised bit of the world, however tiny, which is greater than anyone else's knowledge of that bit, is safe for life. Knowledge grows by infinitesimals, but understanding of the world actually recedes, because the world really is an interacting system.

I argue in this chapter that relations, processes of cognition, pattern and structure are central categories and that SEI must adopt a more synthetic methodology. I will, therefore, in the following pages explore in greater depth new ways of understanding schools as organizations and see how far SEI can be incorporated into the new paradigms and methodologies of Dynamical Systems Theory.

School Effectiveness and School Improvement have, until recently, developed as two separate strands of research. This separation is not really useful or rational. Thankfully in the last few years the two traditions have begun to merge (Davies 1994, Gray *et al.* 1996). Before I review these traditions I must pursue a little further the paradigms and frames of reference, because the intention here is to fuse or synthesize two elements. These are School Effectiveness and Improvement (SEI) on one hand and Dynamical Systems Theory on the other.

I take as my premise the belief that we need a new understanding of how schools *live* as organizations. This will require a new insight into how schools behave as Complex Adaptive Systems (CAS); how they co-evolve, learn, develop and seek to perform their primary tasks as adaptive non-linear feedback networks. Much SEI research has paid too little attention to these dynamic, non-linear elements of schools and has failed to take sufficient cognizance of such vital elements of complex adaptive organizational dynamics as self-organization, feedback cycles and emergence, states of the system control parameters (e.g. rates of information flow, connectivity, variety, levels of anxiety in the system, power differentials) and what Ralph Stacey (1996) refers to as the 'Recessive' or 'Shadow System' and its interrelatedness with the 'Dominant' or 'Legitimate' System. These are concepts that I shall expand upon below.

A great deal of work has been done in this field of the science of complexity, first in the physical sciences (e.g. Axelrod 1984, Bak and Chen 1991, Prigogine and Stengers 1984, Baker and Gollub 1990, Gell-Mann 1994, Gleick 1988, Waldrop 1992, Kauffman 1993, 1995, 2000, R. Lewin 1992, Langton 1986, Lorenz 1995), then in the corporate and business field (Arthur 1989, Sterman 1988, Trippi 1995, Stacey 1993, 1996, 2001, 2002, Morgan 1986), but to a much lesser degree in the field of education (Brodnick and Krafft 1997, Cronbach 1988, Fitz-Gibbon 1996, Fullan 1993, 1999, Morrison 2002).

Ralph Stacey (1996), on whose work I have drawn extensively, describes the current dominant corporate management paradigm in terms of a dominant and guiding question: '*How can we design our organisations so that they will yield successful outcomes?*' (1996: 4). It is fair to say that the SEI movement by and large shares this dominant question as its guiding frame of reference. This simple question that has driven management research and practice for most of the last century is, as Stacey suggests, a source of much stress and anxiety. This basic question leads to a set of linear assumptions that tend inexorably towards states that are in equilibrium and that are predictable. The search is for successful intended outcomes and the focus is upon the formal, legitimate, structural, measurable, manageable and controllable elements of the system. Systems tend to be treated as parts-strung-together. The underlying model is a mechanistic input-process-output system. The unwritten assumption is that 'successful outcomes' are achieved through stable, predictable in-equilibrium organizational states. My proposal is that successful management in the twenty-first century will require careful attention to and management for far-from-equilibrium states that are non-linear, unpredictable, and that allow for and create a special 'space' or 'condition' (located, as some would say, close to chaos[1] or far from equilibrium) where self-organization is maximized while at the same time control is maintained and chaos and rigidity are avoided. I will call this state the 'learning zone' or 'space for creativity'. In these conditions, institutional learning and creativity are maximized.

An important insight of dynamical systems theory is that complex adaptive non-linear systems such as schools operate best when their internal feedback mechanisms are allowed to interact with internal and external environments to generate purpose. This implies not that the external environment plays no part in generating that purpose, but that the system and its environment must co-evolve and the system needs space for self-organization and for creativity. It does mean that attempts to force purposes (interventions) onto non-linear adaptive systems without sensitivity to their natural co-evolutionary dynamics and values of their control parameters (as described above) can be counterproductive. It is to an understanding of these mechanisms and processes of feedback, self-organization and system learning and creativity that the educational world should devote much more attention. I will return to this subject in detail but will first review the current and past developments of SEI research.

School effectiveness research

Signs are beginning to appear that researchers in the field of SEI are realizing that complexity science is an important dimension. So far this has only manifested itself in relatively superficial comment on complexity issues in education. For example, Goldstein and Myers (1997) make some wide acknowledgements of weaknesses in SE research, accepting that 'complexity and context are ignored' and that there is a need for 'a detailed explication of how schools, teachers and other factors interact to produce complexity of relationships that empirical studies are beginning to unearth'.

Fullan (1993, 1999) incorporates some elements of complexity theory into his powerful analysis of educational change management. Fitz-Gibbon (1996) discusses some detailed technicalities of complexity theory in educational contexts and suggests the need for a move away from 'effectiveness' and 'improvement' research focuses to a 'complexity' focus. Since she made this plea the research community has not appeared to move in this direction in any meaningful way. Some more recent discussions of SEI (Morley and Rasool 1999), though acknowledging deep problems associated with SEI, nevertheless make no mention at all of complexity science. It is, however, acknowledged in the preface that 'British schools are now subject to more supervision and intervention than those of any other developed country' (1999: viii).

SEI has been full of exhortation, lists of factors for successful outcomes, and suggested interventions couched within a technical-rational frame. Schooling seems to have been engulfed by a managerialism with high levels of goal- and task-orientation and exhortations to practitioners to try harder at implementing centrally articulated mandates for improvement and successful outcomes. Morley and Rasool (1999: 5) go so far as to say that SEI 'often has quasi-religious connotations, implying lack, deficit or original sin'. They also describe school effectiveness as 'a vast industry, legitimized through public policy, finance and educational research' (1999: 129).

In all this there has been a tendency to ignore and discount the 'complexity of relationships' of Goldstein and Myers, who go on to say that schools are 'complex interactive structures'. However, in the midst of such fleeting references there is little sign of a willingness or ability to understand the consequences for SEI research and the radical change of direction and focus required to move forward.

An understanding and development of dynamical systems theory in educational management and planning can alleviate the stress and frustration that are evident in schools due in part to the earnest pursuit of interventionist, old-paradigm SEI approaches. Development of an understanding of schools as adaptive non-linear feedback networks is a matter of some urgency, and education has much ground to make up in this field compared with the business, legal and corporate worlds.

School Effectiveness and Improvement research has developed in different ways in different parts of the world. It is beyond the scope of this book to review the international literature worldwide. For this reason I will concentrate on the mainstream of research and practice in Europe and North America.

The early stages

The SE movement was triggered, as is well known, by the work on equality of opportunity by James Coleman and his collaborators (Coleman *et al.* 1966) and Christopher Jencks (Jencks *et al.* 1972). Both Coleman and Jencks published pessimistic findings on the potential influence of schools and teachers on students' achievement. Jencks concluded, 'If all (American) high schools were equally effective, differences in attainment would be reduced by less than one percent' (cited by Ouston *et al.* 1979: 3). This was naturally deeply discouraging to policymakers and practitioners in public education. Such negative findings quickly called into question levels of public funding of education, and it became a matter of urgency for policymakers to find some legitimization for large-scale expenditure on mainstream schooling. Therefore, from the very start, the School Effectiveness movement was imbued with deeply political motivations.

In the United States and the United Kingdom, ripostes were swift. Two key studies by Edmonds (1979) in the US and Rutter *et al.* (1979) in the UK set out to examine the evidence and to gain a view on the ability of schools to 'make a difference to students' life chances'. Both studies arrived independently at the conclusion that schools did make a small but important difference to the life chances of their students.

SEI research has progressed through a number of stages and into increasingly sophisticated and ambitious investigations of schools and their effectiveness.

The second stage

The 1980s saw the systematic refining of SE research methodologies, and findings were replicated with students of different ages and in different settings. In the UK this stage had a background of radical change and reform driven by the Conservative government of Margaret Thatcher culminating in the Education Reform Act of 1988. The main elements of the reform agenda were: a national curriculum, locally controlled school budgets, parental choice of school, teacher appraisal and freedom for schools to opt out of local authority control. Perhaps the most dominant theme at this time was the unleashing of the market into public services such as education and health. A typical example of the more sophisticated approach to SE research is a large-scale study of schools in Louisiana (Teddlie, Kirby and Stringfield 1989). In the UK the ILEA conducted large-scale research into its primary schools (Mortimore *et al.* 1988) that confirmed, in the words of the author, 'the central finding of earlier work that schools had different levels of effectiveness'. Such a statement merely confirmed what practitioners already 'knew'. This work also showed that data on prior attainment, social class, gender and race of junior-school entrants were a poor indicator of pupils' likely progress in the ensuing four years. More information was needed on the organizational character of the school in order to make predictions.

It was at this stage that the United Kingdom SE movement highlighted what were termed 'key factors'. Sammons *et al.* (1995) used more than 160 studies to create a list of factors that were said to be key contributors to effective schools. The factors were divided into those associated with academic outcomes and those with social outcomes. The factorial approach was not new. Rutter *et al.* (1979) had identified twenty academic factors and only seven social factors. The United States also saw a search for 'correlates' for effectiveness (Brookover and Lezotte, 1979; Brookover *et al.* 1984).

The third stage

The third stage of SE research running through to the late 1990s saw a shift of focus from SE research towards action research into School Improvement. During this time new empirical studies of effectiveness continued, such as work on secondary school subject departments by Sammons *et al.* (1997). Methodologies became more sophisticated, and the statistical database grew to enormous proportions.

In the United Kingdom, there have been a number of central questions to which SE research has returned again and again:

- Do schools have any effects on students at all?
- Can schools be shown to be consistently effective or ineffective over time?
- Do schools have the same effects on all students?
- Are schools equally effective in dealing with different aspects of students' development?
- What makes schools effective as whole organizations?

SE methodology

SE research starts from a simple premise: if schools make a difference in the life chances of their pupils, what school-based factors account for the differences and what factors account for higher levels of achievement? The search is on to find those school-based qualities that lead to the more successful outcomes. In other words, we have the classical, dominant management paradigm referred to above (Chapter 2): *How can we design our organizations so that they will yield successful outcomes?* This leads to a basic rational-mechanistic methodology of a) ANALYSE external environments and internal capabilities, b) DESIGN organizational structures, practices and behaviours to c) FIT the environments and deliver outputs (Stacey 1996). In today's rapidly changing environments where predictability is impossible due to faster information flows, this methodology in turn leads to anxiety and stress. Stacey (1996: 3) states:

> Our framework, however, defends us against that anxiety using the defence of denial. In other words the framework insists that we must design organizations and intend outcomes, conditioning us to assume that there is no alternative – we simply must foresee and stay in control, for without this there can be no order, only anarchy.

The methodology of SE research is, therefore, conceptually simple but over the years has become statistically so complex that some of it is inaccessible to practitioners. The preferred method is to establish a selection of 'outcomes' as measures of schools' success. A range of intervening variables such as social class, gender, race and prior attainment are allowed for, and the 'surplus' is calculated as a form of 'value-added' that has been contributed by the schools. 'Outputs' have tended to be elements that are most amenable to measurement, such as test scores, exam results and truancy rates.

Some perceived weaknesses of SE research

Davies (1994) points out that 'nearly thirty years of research has not managed to dispel Coleman's initial findings that a large proportion of divergence in pupil achievement is linked to their home environment'. However, in the UK and US school effectiveness seems set to continue to occupy a high profile, associated with policy imperatives to 'raise standards' and 'achieve targets' and in the political context of 'naming and shaming'. Throughout its existence it has been the focus of much political interest, and has been viewed by some as a legitimating device for new policies. Davies (1994, 1997), Pring (1996), Hamilton (1996), Elliot (1996), White and Barber (1997) have recently been critical of SE research, and have drawn responses from SE researchers (Sammons *et al.* 1996, Mortimore and Sammons 1997, Mortimore and Whitty 1997).

The criticisms have centred around three main issues. The first is that SE research has claimed too much for its findings. The second is that SE concentrates on restricted 'cognitive' outcomes of schooling and ignores the many other aspects, which are important but more difficult to measure. The third is that it has supported the process of governmental centralization and the control of education and educational professionals.

Goldstein and Myers (1997: 214) observe pessimistically:

> The school effectiveness research base is used to justify blaming schools for 'failing' on the assumption that because some schools succeed in difficult circumstances the reason others do not must be their own fault. In this scenario complexity and context are ignored. Furthermore some politicians and policymakers have found it possible to deny their role in 'failure' by shifting all the blame onto individual schools.

Other problems associated with SE research and ideology include the following:

1   The selection of the outcomes as measures of school effectiveness is not a neutral matter. As mentioned above, there is a tendency to select what is more easily measurable, such as test and examination results, leaving out a range of important qualitative outcomes such as social awareness, citizenship, ethical values, self-esteem, vocational preparation, leadership development and lifelong learning.
2   There are huge technical difficulties and complexities in describing desirable features of schools in the face of huge variations of circumstances. For example, it is necessary to take into account differences in geographical area, subject groupings, age, gender, abilities and preferred learning styles to mention but a few. SE research takes a reductionist approach in trying to isolate key variables, when in practice the variables are powerfully interactive as dynamical systems theory would be quick to emphasize.
3   Causality is a deep problem for SE research. SE research tries to identify factors associated with desirable outcomes, but it has not always been easy to prove a cause-and-effect relationship. For example, high expectations may be caused by a high-quality intake of pupils rather than itself being a cause of good exam or test scores. Complexity science suggests that, in complex adaptive systems like schools, links between specific action and long-term outcomes are lost. The achievement of intended specific long-term outcomes is highly problematical; only creative and innovative outcomes can emerge. Stacey (1996: 214) asserts clearly:

> Only when their organisation is operating in the stable zone – when they are conducting ordinary management to reinforce what they already do well – will they be able to realise intended long-term outcomes, and only then if the fitness landscape as determined by others stays stable enough for long enough.

Among the most recent and radical critiques of school effectiveness is work carried out in the United Kingdom by Slee, Weiner and Tomlinson (1998). Their main objections are that social class seems to be considered merely as a control variable, not as an important phenomenon and problem in its own right and part of the complex nature of society and education per se. They also argue, as I do in Chapter 4, that the role of power and politics is underestimated and that complexities are ignored in the interests of a managerial approach based upon broad generalizations. Like others mentioned above they criticize the production of 'endless lists of factors to be taken up as reform recipes by the school improvers' (1998: 2) and state that this leads to a naive reductionism upon which neo-conservative educational agendas of efficiency, standards and 'performativity' have been based.

It is clear from this that current SE ideology and practice are out of step with the complexity paradigm. The message to SE research is clear and most unwelcome: only by chance can we actualize specific long-term aims and outcomes in states other than strict stability and equilibrium. Short-term outcomes can be predictable. Ordinary management activity within the formal (legitimate) system can satisfy short-term needs of primary task performance. Members of organizations can influence the values of control parameters. The main control parameters in schools and all other human systems are, as we have seen, *rate of information flow, connectivity, behavioural variety, the level of anxiety that can be contained and degree of power differentials* and how they are used. It is clear that attempting to manage for long-term outcomes is increasingly difficult, but the control parameters can be influenced by managing anxiety levels, the use and distribution of power, the rate of flow of information and the levels of connectivity across the institution.

I do not intend to investigate these perceived weaknesses in detail. My purpose here is to suggest that the SEI movement has been hindered by a failure to recognize an important set of realities requiring a new dominant theoretical framework capable of making sense of dynamical systems in rapidly changing environments. An important dimension is missing that has distorted the whole process. I will now show briefly how the SEI movement has lately shown signs of realizing this. I will review the main findings of School Improvement research and then go on to a more detailed discussion of a systems and complexity approach to SEI.

School improvement

School improvement was famously defined by the OECD-sponsored International School Improvement Project as follows: 'A systematic, sustained effort aimed at change in learning conditions and other related internal conditions in one or more schools, with the ultimate aim of accomplishing educational goals more effectively' (van Velzen *et al.* 1985).

Here we see once again the dominant old management framework based on the question, *How can we design and manage our schools to yield successful outcomes?* The work of the International School Improvement Project did much to increase the profile of School Improvement as an approach to educational change (Hopkins, Ainscow and West 1994). SI shifted the emphasis firmly towards the school as the main locus for change, and it questioned the effectiveness of externally mandated interventionism. Hargreaves and Hopkins (1993: 234) confirm that SI 'implies a very different way of thinking about change than the ubiquitous "top-down" approach so popular with policy makers'.

SI does mark an important move towards understanding schools as systems operating in environments. Hopkins (1996) saw SI as 'the process through which schools adapt external changes to internal purpose'. So there begins to be a recognition that external policy alone cannot deliver the desired 'outcomes'. The decisive locus of change must be within schools. Hopkins (1996: 41) goes on to call for: 'Implementation-friendly policy that is concerned with the process as well as the substance of change at the teacher and school level'.

Slowly and painfully the research and policy communities were groping their way to the end of the cul-de-sac of old management thinking: *How can we manage our schools to yield successful outcomes?* SE was viewed by many teachers as being associated with centralized top-down interventionism, and SI was increasingly seen as teacher- and school-friendly allowing for bottom-up improvement: a rather artificial and unhealthy dualism.

SI research developed a number of focuses that appear to lead towards a more systemic approach to schools and their purposes.

School culture

One of the central themes of the school improvement literature has been the importance of school culture for the processes of change and improvement. This was in many ways a liberating development as it enabled practitioners to get away from the rigours and detail of specific effectiveness factors and concentrate on a more holistic approach. The culture of the school was seen to include interaction and discourses, values and ethos, conscious and unconscious schemas and ways of doing things. All these features are very hard to observe, let alone measure.

The emphasis on school culture led to a number of typologies of different types or stages of school development. Hopkins *et al.* (1994) suggest a four-fold typology: *stuck, promenading, wandering and moving.* Fig. 3.1 illustrates a fivefold typology developed by Stoll and Fink (1996) on the basis of the binaries of *effective–ineffective, improving–declining.*

Again, the move is gradually towards the interactive psychodynamics of schools and organizations, but there seems little understanding or aware-

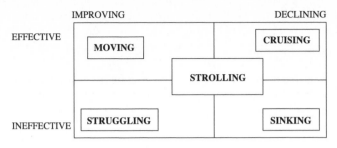

Figure 3.1 Various states of school culture

Source: adapted from Stoll and Fink (1996)

ness of the complexity, unpredictability and dynamics of the complex adaptive system that lie beneath the surface of schools as living entities.

SI researchers quickly acknowledged that culture cannot easily be changed or influenced directly. Certainly any direct attempt to alter the culture of a school is likely to meet with serious problems. This led to a complementary emphasis upon changing structures and thereby influencing the underlying culture of school. Indeed, Hopkins (1996) recognizes that the structures of an institution are often a reflection of its culture – though the opposite is also likely. The UK's Improving the Quality of Education for All (IQEA) project in the 1990s focused a great deal of attention on the relationship between culture and structure in schools.

Inquiry, reflection and the school as a learning organization

The systems thinking on 'The Learning Organization' (Senge 1990, 2000, Argyris 1999) that became fashionable in the 1990s had an impact on SI research. The role of inquiry and reflection among individuals and institutions was stressed. In particular, SI concentrated upon monitoring, evaluation and research – particularly action research among teachers. At last the educational community was beginning to think of change and improvement as a process in which an orientation towards connections and relationships was crucial in order to engender movement, change and learning. *Vision, professional autonomy of teachers, self-accountability, teams and adaptivity* were all highlighted. Fitz-Gibbon (1996: 83–84) came closest to a complexity approach, with a clear call for emphasis on feedback and information systems:

> Self-organizing units can only respond effectively if they have the necessary information. . . . In order to make effective decisions for school improvement we need values (to know in which directions we wish to move) and information. To thrive on the edge of chaos, the system needs the capacity to act in multiple self-organizing, adequately informed, local units, i.e. the capacity to act on the basis of feedback.

It seems, therefore, that by the late 1990s some elementary ideas of complexity theory were entering the SEI discourses, yet very little progress has been made in taking these ideas forward and deepening the debate and research.

I will now move on to a detailed discussion of this highly technical area with a view to moving this field forward and showing its importance to educational research and practice.

Dynamical systems theory and schools

I intend to try to transpose or map some of the emerging theories and understandings of dynamical systems theory onto an understanding of schools. In so doing I hope to demonstrate that it is possible vastly to increase the creativity, energy, learning and fitness-for-purpose of schools and other human systems. This work involves crossing an important watershed, as I will explain. In a sense we will try to understand schools using biological, systemic and psychological metaphors and thus we may escape from the mechanistic (stable equilibrium) approaches that are still prevalent. In describing the essentials of dynamical systems I will of necessity use rather bloodless technical and theoretical language. This does not mean that we can afford to lose sight of the realities of human situations and interactions, which are full of everyday difficulties and possibilities. I will root the theory, which you will find is full of life, in everyday examples in following chapters.

There is a new synthesis of thinking on the fascinating question of life and its attributes of self-organization, variation, mutation, autopoiesis (see below) and dazzling complexity and simplicity. Life and living systems can be studied at all levels: micro-organisms, animal and plant life, social systems, human systems and ecosystems.

The realms of complexity theory and human organizational dynamics are vast technical fields. I will attempt to outline the essentials of the theory insofar as they relate to and illuminate the practice of leadership in schools. In this exercise I am greatly indebted to Ralph Stacey (1996), who has done remarkable and detailed work in aligning complexity theory and organizational psychodynamics with the management of human organizations. Central to what I hope to achieve is a description of the control parameters that, as it were, 'tune' the 'operating frequency' of a system to a state of optimal creativity and innovation, which has been described as occurring in the 'phase transition' between stable and unstable states or 'far from equilibrium' states.

Theoretical strands

My work has drawn upon a number of theoretical traditions, which I have collectively named Dynamical Systems Theory. These include:

Complexity Theory, from which I have developed the concepts of *system control parameters, self-organization* and *attractors*.

Organizational Learning Theory, based upon work by Argyris (1999) and popularized by authors such as Senge (1990). This deals with *theories-in-use, concepts of single- and double-loop learning* and with *models of system learning.*

Organizational Psychodynamics developed by Bion (1991) at the Tavistock Institute in London and at the A.K. Rice Institute in the USA. This develops important ideas concerning two systems within organizations: the *legitimate system* and the *shadow system.*

Schools as complex dynamical systems

Complex reality is formalized most effectively using the concept of the system. A system can be defined as a group of interacting, interdependent elements that form a complex whole. Systems are further defined by their boundaries. Outside the boundary is the system's environment, and 'boundary permeability' is the degree to which the system interacts with its external environment through the exchange of energy, information and other resources. In the case of a school these will be in the form of students, money, information and materials. The degree of 'boundary permeability' determines the extent to which a system is described as relatively closed or open. A closed system functions independently of its environment. System dynamics and systems thinking, popularized by Senge (1990, 2000), is the study of feedback mechanisms of complex systems and how these mechanisms generate patterns of behaviour within the system and its overall behaviour. When systems behave in a linear fashion they are easy to describe and their function over time is easy to predict. An obvious example is a swinging pendulum or a clock. Some forms of industrial manufacturing in the past used to be modelled on a linear, machine-like model in which machine and worker seemed to be linked into a unified, linear, clockwork and predictable system. Schools in the nineteenth and twentieth centuries seemed to pick up some of these linear, systemic characteristics. I will be concerned here with schools as systems which behave in a non-linear manner and are therefore not easy to describe and whose function over time is difficult to predict.

Systems are, as we have seen, composed of 'agents' that interact with each other in a cyclical and iterative manner. These processes of interaction create the system's internal environment. Systems never exist in isolation, so agents also interact with external agents and systems, and this process helps create the external environment. Systems have a tendency to 'fractal' self-similarity across all scales and between levels of organization. Schools, like any other human organization, develop and change over time largely through an internal and external interactive process involving feedback

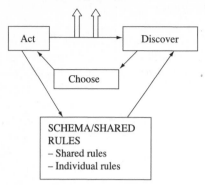

CONSEQUENCES

Figure 3.2 Basic feedback process in a human system: mode of system cognition in a complex dynamical system (based on Stacey 1996)

loops. Until quite recently not much was known in detail about this process. Stacey (1996) describes the basic feedback process in human systems as a three-part process:

1   *Discover* The process of sensing and interacting with other agents or parts within the organization as well as with its external environment.
2   *Choose* A response to those states encountered in the process of discovering. This response is conditioned by a set of rules or 'schema' which may either be universal or specific or a mixture of both.
3   *Act* On the basis of the sensing and choosing an action takes place and of course action taken by an agent has an impact on other agents in the system.

This basic unit of system process is depicted in Fig. 3.2.

The three essential elements of the cyclical processes of system cognition can be expanded upon as follows:

Discover

Discovery is the process of gathering information and making sense of situations and it is the basis upon which choices are made. Each agent in a system is constantly picking up signals and information, and it constantly examines the state of other agents and systems and their environments. This information is used to make valid meanings.

Choose

Choice is very complex. Agents choose what to discover and how to act on the basis of their discovery and its meaning. Agents choose on the basis of schemas (both specific to an individual and shared by the system as a whole), which are sets of rules making meanings and guiding behaviour.

Act

An agent acts in accordance with its discoveries and choices as explained above. Every act impinges upon other agents, causing them to respond. This sets up an iterating interchange or set of feedback loops.

Schemas

Agents function through the use of *internal models* or *schemas* (Gell-Mann 1994). A schema is created or modified as an agent gains experience through the processes of *discovering*, *choosing* and *acting*. As the agents gain experience they abstract 'regularities' from the randomness within the experience and begin to form internal models that describe these regularities. Agents may construct a number of internal models or schemas for an experience, and over time the recognized patterns and regularities become schemas through a process known as *compression* by which experience is abstracted. Often these schemas consist of a set of rules by which agents describe events or behaviours (*discover*), predict future events or behaviours (*choose*) and carry out present behaviours (*act*). In a school setting each student and teacher will have many schemas. For example, a student will have schemas determining how to interact with a particular teacher, subject, friend, and type of test or situation. This student will continually create and modify schemas in the light of continuing interaction with teachers for instance. Individual schemas are also modified and dictated by (and also actively influence) the prevailing culture or theory-in-use.

There are two types of schema. *Individual schemas* are rules, codes and patterns of behaviour, mental models, operational rules and evaluation rules. These are used as guides to action and choice. *Shared schemas* involve hierarchical, bureaucratic, ideological and cultural rules. Schemas, therefore, can be viewed as scripts or rules or models that shape and guide behaviour. In individuals they grow and develop over a lifetime. Shared schemas often take the form of explicit organizational rules and procedures, but also they can be contained within a shared organizational culture. In time many of them become unconscious, but they continue to exert a powerful influence over behaviour. Much work has been done on human behavioural schemas by psychologists and especially in the field of transactional analysis (Baddeley 1990, Berne 1964, Kuhn 1970, Huff 1990, Argyris and Schon 1978, Argyris 1999). An essential element of schemas are 'IF, THEN' rules. For example, 'IF you threaten me, THEN I will attack you' or, 'IF it rains on Friday, THEN I will not watch the soccer match'. A detailed analysis of schemas is beyond the scope of this work,

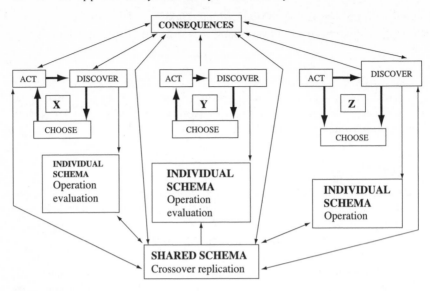

Figure 3.3 Complex adaptive system with three or more agents

Some systems exercise cloning replication where a set of replication instructions guides agents to copy exactly its operating and replicating rules in order to create a new agent. In this diagram crossover replication involves an agent finding a mate and copying half of its own rules or schema and adding them to half of the other agents rules thus producing much greater diversity of schemas through cross-fertilization. This form of cross-fertilization can take place in genes, computer bit strings and in human ideas and behaviours

Source: Adapted from Stacey (1996)

but they are nevertheless a key element of the cyclical process of feedback, evaluation, action and reaction that creates the internal environment of an organization. A detailed description and analysis of theories-in-use is developed below.

An expanded version of a complex adaptive system is illustrated in Fig. 3.3.

Psychodynamics and creativity in groups

An understanding of human behaviour in groups is vital to our understanding of the 'creative state' or 'learning zone'. Bion (1991) asserts that any group of people normally come together for a specific primary task. There is simultaneously a parallel or shadow group or what Bion called a 'basic assumption' group. This refers to the general background emotional atmosphere in which a group operates. Bion postulates that groups operate simultaneously at both levels:

- *The work group*. This is the manifest level of the group's performance and it is devoted to the primary and legitimate tasks of the group. This is readily understood by group members. In schools, the legitimate or primary task consists of those aims, processes and outcomes that the community and stakeholders have agreed upon. They are the purposes formerly laid down in charters, prospectuses, mission statements or required by law. They form the overt and explicit purpose and aims of the organization or group.
- *The basic assumption group*. The basic assumption group process is about the group acting *as though* the group members had made the basic and shared assumption that the group had met to do one of the following things:

  a) Depend on someone or something outside themselves (either within or outside the group). This is *basic assumption dependence.*
  b) Fight or flee from something: *basic assumption fight/flight.*
  c) Pair or mate: *basic assumption pairing.*

According to Bion, the prevalent basic assumption provides the emotional energy for everything that happens within the group, and it has a fundamental influence on the norms and roles adopted within the group. When tamed or harnessed in the interests of the group's primary tasks or activities, it helps and energizes the group. When it runs counter to the group's primary task or activities, it saps and diverts energy from the task performance and makes the group dysfunctional.

Dealing with basic assumption dependence is the stock-in-trade of the teaching profession, though few are aware of this. For example, a group may have a tendency to depend on someone, thus leading to a state of dependency. Normal levels of basic assumption behaviour are beneficial and can enhance group primary tasks. For example, a background level of dependency can assist learning in a classroom. However, if it comes to dominate the group it will make learning very difficult. In general, domination by basic assumption behaviour occurs when the normal structures are removed and leadership negated. This causes anxiety to increase and it then becomes difficult for the group to be creative. One of the fascinations of TV programmes devoted to groups of individuals living as castaways on remote and difficult islands is precisely the phenomenon of the rise of this basic-assumption type behaviour among the group when the normal props of 'civilized' home life are removed. Raw and dangerous emotions tend to be let loose. This is what we might call the *Lord of the Flies* effect. The point about this is that those emotions are not absent in everyday life. They are just more hidden beneath the surface and are quite capable of rising to the surface in schools and elsewhere if the institutional emotions are not well understood and managed by wise leaders.

Although it is a highly specialized and technical field, I feel it is worth briefly describing some of the essentials of a psychodynamic approach to organizations. From Table 3.1 it should be clear how important the creative state is and how it relates to other system states seen in a psychodynamic perspective. The combination of dynamical systems theory and psychodynamics gives a powerful theoretical framework for understanding organizations in dynamic contexts.

In Table 3.1 the central column represents the creative state or 'learning zone' phase transition. Perhaps the most notable feature of the creative state is that it is full of paradoxes and ambiguity. On the left in Table 3.1 is the chaotic and unstable state that tends to disintegration and is filled

Table 3.1 Characteristics of systems in different states

Individual		
Paranoid/schizoid position	*Normal/'depressive' position*	*Defensive/conformist position*
Disintegration	Play	Conformist
Psychotic fantasy	Use of transitional objects	Concrete reality
Splitting	Paradoxes	Denial
Projecting	Creative	Ossification
Neurotic	Fluid/flexible	Stability
Group and individual learning models		
Opposite Model I	*Model II*	*Model I*
Basic assumption behaviour	Shifting leadership	Rigid hierarchy
Psychotic fantasy	Mature followership	Fixed rules, routines and
Disintegration	Ambiguity and paradox	rituals
	Creativity and rich	Defensive behaviour
	learning	Stability
		Ossification
Organizational states		
Paranoid/schizoid position	*Creative state*	*Defensive conformist state*
Uncontained anxiety	State of flux	Sparsely connected
Unconscious fantasies	Balance of change and	Conformist
Weak formal or	order	Anxiety avoided
legitimate system	Anxiety simultaneously	Colludes with legitimate
Highly interconnected	allowed and contained	system
and diverse. Highly active	Creative tension with	Quiescent shadow system
shadow system	legitimate system	

with uncontained anxieties and emotions. On the right is the stable rigid state that tends to ossification and sterility and keeps emotions firmly underground. It should be noted that the use of the term *depressive position* does not mean 'depressive' in the popular sense of that word but is a technical term developed in Kleinian psychoanalytic theory, which I will not develop further here. Simply put, it represents a normal and balanced human personality.

Paradoxical features of the creative state

- Information flows freely and is retained.
- Schemas display both diversity and conformity.
- Agents are richly but not too richly connected.
- Behaviour is both predictable and unpredictable, patterned and irregular.
- Systems are both patterned and irregular with a mixture of order and disorder.
- Competition and cooperation coexist.
- Creativity and destruction coexist.
- Destruction occurs through a process of positive amplifying feedback that breaks down symmetries.
- Creativity occurs through self-organization which leads to new forms of emergent order.
- There is a tension between sustaining and defending the status quo (dominant legitimate system) and replacing or subverting it (recessive shadow system).
- The system modulates and fluctuates to draw the system simultaneously away from equilibrium and back towards equilibrium through a process of canalization.
- There is stability of pattern and shape and archetypal form but instability in the detailed actualization of form and outcome.

Human individual paradoxes in the learning zone

- Love and hate the same object
- Urge to separate and individuate as well as to fuse and lose oneself
- Destructive urge and creative urge
- Desire for safety, security and comfort as well as desire for the exciting and unknown
- Desire for rational, functional and factual against longing for the aesthetic, emotional and sacred.

Theories-in-use and learning models

The group learning models depicted in the central column in Table 3.1 refer to the ideas of theory-in-use and single- and double-loop learning

(Argyris and Schon 1978, Argyris 1990, 1999). This work is of singular importance to the idea of the learning organization. These ideas are based upon the understanding that humans design actions to achieve 'intended consequences and monitor themselves to learn whether their actions are effective' (Argyris 1999: 241). This process requires people to construct a simplified representation of their environment. This relates to the 'IF, THEN' rules that I suggested above. Rather than construct new models in every instance, individuals develop a sort of repertoire of rules, schemas and strategies to help guide their actions as they seek to solve problems or act in new situations. Argyris refers to these 'programs' as *'theories of action'*. There are two types of *theories of action*: espoused theories, which an individual *claims* to use, and theory-in-use that they actually use in practice.

Two basic theories-in-use are identified. These are:

1 Model I: theory-in-use

This is essentially a defensive reasoning strategy that is almost ubiquitous in management circles. Argyris observed that Model I was the theory-in-use of virtually everyone he had studied. Model I is driven by four main governing variables:

a)   Achieve the purpose as the actor defines it
b)   Win; do not lose
c)   Suppress negative feelings
d)   Emphasize rationality.

This is a model of behaviour in which the individual seeks to remain in unilateral control over situations and people. Characteristic ways of behaving in this mode include much covert and opaque decision-making, much face-saving activity and the discouraging of open discussion and enquiry. This form of behaviour leads to escalating errors, and learning is stuck in the realms of 'what is acceptable' (p. 243). Overall effectiveness and deep learning steadily decrease.

There is a sort of flip side to this Model I, known as *Opposite Model I*, whose governing variables are:

a)   Participation of all in decision-making
b)   Everyone wins; no one loses
c)   Express feelings
d)   Suppress the cognitive, intellective aspects of action.

(Argyris 1999)

2 *Model II: theory-in-use*

Most people espouse Model II theory-in-use, but it is very rare actually to see it in use. The governing variables of Model II are:

a) Valid information
b) Free and informal choice
c) Internal commitment.

Model II is characterized by strategies that involve sharing decision-making and control and open decision, enquiry and advocacy. There is much less defensive interpersonal behaviour. There is more freedom of choice and a culture that is more conducive to risk-taking. There is much more probability of double-loop learning, and issues that were previously hidden and 'undiscussable' will be surfaced and addressed. Assumptions will be tested and, where necessary, amended. 'Self-sealing' processes will be challenged. Perhaps the most potent feature of Model II scenarios is that participants are increasingly seen as *originators* and able to experience *high personal causation*. This has a vital impact on morale and creativity.

It is clear from this that Model I, Opposite Model I and Model II learning patterns relate very precisely to our other mappings of system control parameters and the psychodynamics of basic assumption and work group behaviours. Model I reflects the static values of system control parameters such as *information flow and quality, connectivity, variety of schemas, power differential and anxiety*. Opposite Model I represents very high (chaotic) levels of these values, and Model II represents a critical modulating of these values at optimal levels. (See Table 6.1 in Chapter 6.)

Autopoiesis and dynamical systems

We move now to another very important set of understandings about how complex living systems work to maintain their identities. Much important work has been done in recent years on the concept of cognition that has caused a profound change in our understanding, not only of cognition itself but also of mind and the definition of living systems. Two remarkable Chilean scientists, Maturana and Varela (1980), arrived at the astonishing conclusion that the autopoietic process of living systems is itself cognition. This is sometimes referred to as the Santiago Theory. The work of Maturana and Varela is momentous in philosophical terms because it is a major step towards overcoming the Cartesian duality of mind and matter. At last mind and matter can be viewed as elements of the same phenomenon of living systems and not as separate and distinct categories. The Santiago Theory sees mind not as a discrete entity but the very *process* of cognition *whether or not the system has a brain*. The three key criteria of living systems are:

1   *Pattern of organization:* that is, the configuration of relationships that create the system's environment and essential characteristics;
2   *Structure:* that is, the physical make-up of the particular system, its substantive individual parts;
3   *Process:* the way in which the system continually 'makes itself' and embodies itself in its own unique pattern of organization. This process is known as *autopoiesis* or self-making.

Maturana and Varela understood for the first time that cognition *is* the process of life or self-making and that cognition can occur without a brain,[2] because it is the very process by which any living system 'makes itself' and that requires cycles of feedback either sophisticated – as described above – or simple as in a simple deterministic feedback loop. Kapra (1996: 171) expresses the importance of these insights as follows:

> The interdependence of *pattern* and *structure* allows us to integrate two approaches to the understanding of nature that have been separate and in competition throughout Western science and philosophy. The interdependence of *process* and *structure* allows us to heal the split between mind and matter that has haunted our modern era ever since Descartes.

Whether human systems can be described as autopoietic has been debated at length. In human systems, language plays a definitive role and is the critical element in the emergence of human culture and consciousness. Therefore, because of the power of concepts, ideas and symbols of human thought, human systems operate in both a physical and a social domain. In other words, human systems can be seen as both biological and social entities. Luhmann (1990) decisively develops the idea of social autopoiesis with the idea that, 'social systems use communication as their particular mode of autopoietic reproduction'.

A basic characteristic of autopoietic systems is that parts are definable through their *relations* within the system that they play a dynamic role in forming by relating to both the whole as a unity and to other parts as constituent components. It is not possible to define the elements of a living system by the analysis of the whole into its parts, because the process of analysis destroys the very *relations* that make the parts definable as effective components of an autopoietic whole. Needless to say, old-style reductionism ignores this fundamental fact. It is the process of *relating* that renders the whole far more than the sum of the parts.

Maturana and Varela (1980) were unable to agree on whether or not human societies are biological systems and, therefore, whether they can legitimately be described as autopoietic; so they remain largely silent on the subject. However in the book's introduction (1980: 70), Stafford Beer boldly asserts that they are:

Any cohesive social institution is an autopoietic system – because it survives, because its method of survival answers the autopoietic criteria, and because it may change its entire appearance and its apparent purpose in the process. As examples I list: firms and industries, schools and universities, clinics and hospitals, professional bodies, departments of state and whole countries!

An example may be given here to illustrate the nature of autopoiesis. If a whole school goes on an extended trip, it remains a school in spite of its changed location and circumstances. The school, as a system, is constantly making itself, and its essential organizational relations are invariant: the head remains the head, the staff the staff, the classes the classes and the essential organization is maintained. It is constantly recreating itself and maintaining its generic and individual networks, patterns and dynamics that establish its identity as a school. At the beginning of a new year, older students have left, new ones have arrived, some staff changes may have been made and possibly significant curricular changes have occurred. Nevertheless the parts continue to create the whole and vice versa in a process of autopoietic identity-making. An autopoietic system such as a school is able to withstand considerable deformation of its domain while maintaining its identity and holding its organizational relations constant. Therefore it follows that autopoietic systems are 'homeostatic' and as such their own organization is the *variable* which they hold as *constant*. If, however, the organization of the system changes, then it loses its identity and either disintegrates or becomes an entity of a different kind.

It should also be noted that it is possible for a system to be autopoietic in its own domain and at the same time allopoietic when approached from the 'next level up'.[3] It may therefore be asserted provisionally that agents in the wider environment such as policymakers and researchers, who are themselves elements within their own autopoietic domains (government departments and universities), have tended to treat schools (the next level down) as allopoietic systems. Maybe herein lies a part of the problem of effectiveness, creativity and morale. We need to investigate closely these interjunctions and dynamics at different levels to find ways of allowing a natural interconnection between systems and their environments. Traditional ideas on organization theory have emphasized the idea that change originates in the environment, with organizations viewed as open systems interacting with their environment to process inputs into outputs (Morgan 1986). This is very much the model adopted in SEI. Such a view is challenged by autopoiesis theory, which questions the validity of distinctions between a system and its environment. Through processes of *autonomy, circularity and self-reference in organizationally closed systems*, the system interacts with its environment in a mode that is in reality a reflection and part of its own self-referential processes. This is to say that a system's environment is really a part of itself.

This theory may seem very strange to those who are used to traditional thinking about organizations as open and essentially linear and deterministic.

Systems are nested within larger systems. A system, for example a school, can be a component within another autopoietic system, for example a local education authority. A process of recursion dynamically braids all in constantly fluctuating autopoietic homeostasis. Given this flexible, fluid and homeostatic processing, new understandings and approaches are called for from managers, researchers and policymakers.

Furthermore, the larger system (LEA, government, society) may cause and define external and independent events or 'interventions', which cause perturbations in the embedded smaller systems (schools). Therefore, one might view these events as *inputs* and the compensating changes of the lesser systems – among which will be the underlying drive to maintain their organizational relations – as *outputs*. In other words, the larger system is causing the lesser to be treated as allopoietic. In this case, Maturana and Varela (1980: 82) accept that an autopoietic system can be integrated into a larger system as a component allopoietic system 'without any alteration in its autopoietic organisation'.

Autopoiesis theory has been applied to social systems (Von Krogh and Vicari 1993) and to legal systems (Luhmann 1990). There is also a growing interest in and acceptance of autopoiesis in management literature (Morgan 1986, Roos 1997). The debate on how autopoiesis can or should be applied to social systems is ongoing (Zeleny 1980, 1981, Ulrich and Probst 1984, Mingers 1994). Johan Roos (1997) concludes: 'The nexus between complex adaptive systems theory and autopoiesis theory has brought forth the foundation of a language to further explore managerial issues that remain unresolved when looked at through conventional strategic management and organisational studies lenses.'

In the face of the highly technical debate about the application of autopoiesis to social systems, perhaps the best approach is to leave the esoteric debate to one side and to work with the non-controversial aspects of the theory. It is widely accepted that autopoietic theory provides plentiful concepts and principles for application and experimentation. Such applications have been made in the fields of law (Teubner 1988, Luhmann 1990), accounting and the family.

The implications of dynamical systems theory for educational management and leadership

If the new dynamical systems paradigm came to dominate educational management and leadership, a radically new agenda would develop. The controlling question, as we have seen, is *How can we design our schools to yield successful outcomes?* This approach has been underpinned by two basic ideas:

1   Successful schools should be encouraged to operate in stable equilibrium states;
2   It is possible to intend specific outcomes with some degree of certainty.

SEI has tried consistently to link a set of specific causes with measurable, predictable and desirable outcomes.

A dynamical systems framework views schools as systems whose optimal operating states are far from equilibrium where the link between cause and longer-term outcome cannot be established. It is therefore difficult to establish a direct causal link between specific types of planning and decision-making and desired outcomes.

The educational (SEI) meta-paradigm has been driven by an orthodox management approach, which analyses organizations using ruthless abstraction and reductionism.

I have explored some of the essential elements of dynamical systems theory in the belief that it can contribute powerfully to the management and delivery of quality education in schools and, above all, can create the context for powerful creativity, meaning and moral purpose. The heart of my thesis can be stated as follows:

- The traditional stable state (dominant) framework or paradigm based upon rational, technical, linear, mechanistic approaches is inadequate for complex systems. Its key focus is upon substance, structure and predictable outcomes. SEI has been operating mainly within this dominant frame of reference.
- This orthodox approach leads to a search for stable equilibrium states and assured outcomes through 'technical/rational' interventions. This tends to encourage centralized systems of control and information.
- In times of rapid change and huge information connectivity, steady-state, equilibrium, linear solutions are less and less effective.

So a new approach is required to revive and energize our understanding of how our schools work. Policymakers, practitioners and researchers are increasingly exploring a systems approach based upon dynamical systems theory, the key elements of which include the following:

- Schools are complex dynamical systems and as such are subject to the 'laws' governing such systems. They are non-linear, dynamic, adaptive entities whose environments are generated through iterated feedback processes leading to system cognition. Their specific changes are unpredictable. Like other similar non-linear complex systems they find their point of greatest pattern, shape and creativity as well (paradoxically) as stability at a critical phase state far from equilibrium.
- Dynamical systems can occupy three basic states:

1   *Stable, equilibrium states*, which lead to ossification and sterility.
2   *Unstable chaotic and random states* which tend towards disintegration.
3   A *far-from-equilibrium phase transition* sometimes referred to as the *creative state* or the 'edge of chaos'. Here vast variety, novelty, creativity and system pattern and learning are possible.

- Complex dynamical systems are subject to control parameters:

  a) *Rate of information flow*. This refers to the amount and quality of relevant information of all sorts that is available within the system. Is the school hierarchy secretive or open? Who knows what, and what use is made of information in the pursuit of agreed outcomes?
  b) *Connectivity*. This is processes of engagement and involvement between individuals and groups. This engagement or *connectivity* is often in the form of affective ties such as loyalty, affection and collegiality, but can also take the dysfunctional forms of intrigue, disruption, political strife and bickering.
  c) *Variety and diversity*. A rich variety of practice and behaviour without too much latitude is conducive to creativity. Too much freedom can lead to anarchic and random conditions. Too little freedom leads to excessive conformity, which stifles creativity.
  d) *Power differentials*. This is the degree to which responsibility is delegated to provide a wide range of centres of influence. Systems can range from highly centralized and autocratic structures to totally devolved structures of power. The former leads to the strangulation of creativity through over-centralization, the latter to immobilization through a lack of an effective decision-making process.
  e) *Anxiety levels*. This is perhaps the most crucial of the control parameters. All change and much new 'actionable' learning brings increases in levels of anxiety. This anxiety is an outcome of increases in the levels of the other four control parameters.

Table 3.2 illustrates the five system control parameters and the three system states that they bear upon. The system control parameters are a complex interaction of a huge variety of influences and forces, and they are a crucial element in the emergence of the creative state in human organizations. When control parameters reach optimal values, the system moves into the phase transition that leads to great novelty, variety, pattern and creativity. *Below* the critical values, and systems will be stuck in the stable zone. *Above* the critical values, and systems will be pushed into highly unstable states that will tend to chaos and disintegration. Psychodynamic theory suggests that the level of anxiety that can be maintained and held in the system is the most important parameter for human systems. Creativity seems to require some level of anxiety and stress, probably because creative states

Table 3.2 System control parameters and system states

System control parameters
QUALITY AND RATE OF INFORMATION FLOW
CONNECTIVITY
VARIETY OF BEHAVIOURAL SCHEMAS
POWER DIFFERENTIALS
ANXIETY LEVELS

System states		
RIGID	CREATIVE	CHAOTIC

thrive on play, paradox and ambiguity. It is therefore necessary not to avoid anxiety but to find ways of accommodating it in creative and tolerable ways.

There is an urgent need to rethink what organizations are all about and also for detailed work on the processes of system learning and cognition. This means exploring ways of enabling schools to learn how to learn through what is known in systems theory as 'double-loop' learning. Double-loop learning (Fig. 3.4) is the way a system adapts its behaviour and processes in response to stimuli in its internal and external environments. It takes place through a mechanism involving changing its schemas. Single-loop learning or processing (Fig. 3.4) takes place when a system uses its existing schemas to adapt to changing circumstances without the need to change its schemas. Double-loop learning or processing is complex and non-linear and results in innovation, creativity and novelty.

The really challenging part of this for educational managers and leaders is the psychological leap of accepting that these qualities and states of learning, pattern and emergent properties cannot be externally mandated or imposed through old-style bureaucracies. System learning and creativity must be seen primarily as an emergent quality. Longer-term outcomes are unpredictable, but the overall shape or 'attractor' is relatively stable. Leaders therefore need to understand the need to create contexts and system states in which deeper (double-loop) learning can take place. This may mean deliberately allowing instability to occur, in which new patterns of behaviour and bifurcations to new attractors can take place.

Very little work has been done on 'attractors' in social organizations, although it is a crucial and central concept in complexity science. Briefly, an attractor is a state of behaviour that a system settles into. Equilibrium states have 'normal' attractors of single or point oscillation. A pendulum has a point attractor. A thermostat has a periodic attractor. The term 'strange attractor' applies to systems in low-dimensional chaos.

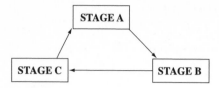

Single-loop process

Single-loop-learning. The system uses its schema and operating rules to detect and correct error in a simple homeostatic process. This is the type of learning that occurs in the circular processes of discover–choose–act described above. No change of schema occurs. The system simply maintains its state.

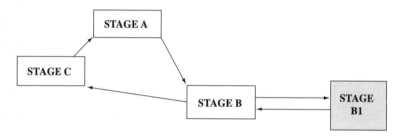

Double-loop process

Double-loop-learning involves a complex process of reflecting upon a situation and changing patterns of behaviour and operating rules and schema.

Stage A   – sensing and scanning the environment or neighbourhood
Stage B   – comparison of this information against schema and operating rules
Stage B1 – questioning the schema concerning their validity and appropriateness
Stage C   – action in the light of sensing and evaluation against schema

Figure 3.4 Single- and double-loop learning processes

Source: adapted from Morgan (1997)

There are four basic kinds of 'attractors' with associated patterns of feedback. The four 'attractors' are:

1   *Point attractor*, such as a pendulum swinging back and forth and eventually stopping at a point.
2   *Periodic attractor*. Give the pendulum a clockwork spring to compensate for friction and inertia, and the pendulum now has a limited cycle in its 'phase space'. The periodic attractor portrays processes that repeat themselves.
3   *Torus attractor*. This looks like a doughnut. The torus attractor depicts systems that stay in a confined area but wander about in that area.

4 *Strange attractor.* The strange attractor depicts systems that are stable, confined, and yet never do exactly the same thing twice, like schools and weather systems. They never repeat their trajectory or behaviour exactly. Each event, each interaction, each end-state, each process is never precisely identical to any other. The most famous strange attractor is the 'Lorenz attractor', whose appearance in that author's 1967 book marked the start of chaos theory. It is a marvellously shaped series of spirals with two bifurcating wings resembling a butterfly.

The first three of these attractors are not associated with chaos because they are fixed or linear attractors.

Stacey (1996) describes the strange attractor as an archetype of potential behaviour:

> The strange attractor is an archetype, a potential pattern of behaviour that has the stability of boundaries and shape, that is, general qualitative features. However, actualisation of that archetype is unpredictable: the particular form that will be realised will depend upon the precise experience of a system over time. The chaos archetype is an irregular or fractal potential pattern whose actualisation occurs through a process in which the system flips autonomously between negative and positive feedback, providing its own internal constraint.
>
> The chaos attractor is paradoxical. It is the simultaneous presence of stability in archetypal or dispositional form and instability in specific actualisation. Chaos is also the only state in which a system is capable of novelty and endless variety because the other attractors, the archetypes of stability and instability, consist of repetition in which the actualisation always coincides with the archetype. Chaos is, therefore, an archetype of novelty, creativity, innovation, and surprise.
>
> In a simple way, one might think of the strange attractor chaos as a phase transition between stability and instability. This will be a useful approximation when we return to human systems, but strictly speaking it is not correct. In the march to chaos described above, a system bifurcates continually until it reaches the strange attractor. Just before it does so, it may pass through a phase transition in which global and short-term order coexists with chaos. This is the true phase transition, described as *the edge of chaos*.

This explanation of attractors shows how systems can behave in extremely complex ways and at the same time have very simple internal structures and rules (Gleick 1988, Stewart 1989, Ruelle 1993).

One of the most potent aspects of a dynamical systems approach to school leadership is that, in the 'edge of chaos' phase transition (creative state) where the chaos archetype holds sway, small but precise and critical changes or initiatives can cause major and transforming results (high leverage). This is known as Sensitive Dependence on Initial Conditions (SDIC). Such a change or initiative, when implemented in the stable equilibrium state, would have little or no effect. To put it another way, the transforming change that can be triggered so easily by such a minimal input in the creative state or 'edge of chaos' state is totally out of reach in the stable state. Traditional management appears to be seeking these mega-transformations without a full realization that they can only be delivered and sustained in the phase transition states close to chaos and far-from-equilibrium. In a sense, therefore, the traditional SEI approach is trying to harvest the fruit before it is ripe. Our gardening metaphor once again comes into its own. Creativity has to be cultivated. The system must be nudged, guided and navigated through careful modulation of the key control parameters into the creative state where the chaos archetype holds sway. In this state, which can take a long time to cultivate, there is stability of archetypal form and instability in actualization that allows for and generates great novelty, innovation and surprise.

In so far as the phase transition at the edge of chaos takes time to develop, it is likely that change in this mode will take the form of a 'punctuated equilibrium'. Long periods of apparent stability will be punctuated with bursts of great creativity, complexity and novelty.

The key questions for school leaders are therefore:

- How and to what extent can this major field of dynamical systems theory be incorporated into the management and delivery of education?
- Is it possible to measure and modulate the control parameters in such a way as to facilitate the navigation of institutions into the creative state phase transition?
- What are the essential principles of system design that can maximize system learning and creativity? How is it possible to create Model II learning environments and theories-in-use?
- What are the design principles that best allow schools to interact and co-evolve with each other and their environments? In particular, how can societal and governmental expectations be accommodated with a dynamical systems approach to the system as a whole?

More specific and technical issues will require detailed and long-term research. These may include the following:

- The nature of attractors in schools
- Information redundancy and its importance for maintaining flexibility and adaptivity in complex systems
- System cognition and its optimization through new management
- Homeostatic mechanisms in schools as autopoietic entities

- Ways of attaining high leverage transformation and change through minimal inputs or interventions in the creative state
- Dynamical systems theory and psychodynamics for classroom management and pupil learning
- Professional development and dynamical systems theory
- Dynamical systems theory and school inspection.

Stacey (1996) sums up the situation clearly:

> A complex adaptive systems approach to understanding organisations offers, not a guarantee of success – there is no such thing – but a more useful framework for making sense of experience, reflecting, and thus potentially designing more effective actions. . . . I suggest that these new efforts, making up the science of complexity, provide an overall framework for pulling together many existing building blocks in the literature of management and organisation into a new way of approaching organisational life. . . . I believe that this new way, which is built firmly upon a psychodynamic approach, provides a more useful way of making sense of life in organisations than the stable equilibrium paradigm that currently dominates attempts to understand the problems of managing organisations. I am not suggesting that the science of complexity provides us with a new set of comprehensive predictions for managing and organising. I am suggesting that it provides a framework for making sense of what we have been doing all along.

The practical workings out of this framework of dynamical systems theory is explored in the following chapters, with practical examples illustrating leadership and management issues in highly unpredictable and turbulent environments full of all the quirks and unpredictabilities to be expected in real-world situations.

Notes

1 Chaos is a technical term used in complexity science, which does not have the same meaning as the popular notion of chaos. Low-dimensional chaos indicates a state of behaviour in a system that has global structure but is unpredictable in detail and specifics over the longer term. High-dimensional chaos displays very little structure. It represents system behaviour that is close to randomness.
2 Difficulties are often encountered in grasping this idea because it is easy to confuse cognition in this systemic sense with thoughtful reflection, which is a peculiarly human capacity involving language, ideas and symbols.
3 *Autopoietic* means processes interlaced in the specific form of a network of production of parts or agents. This dynamic and ever-changing network constantly and precisely constitutes the whole as a unity. *Allopoietic* means systems that have as their product or output something different from themselves. *Autopoietic systems* are autonomous; *allopoietic systems* are not autonomous.

4 Micro-politics
Understanding the shadow system

Introduction

It is a truism to say that schools and colleges, like all other human organizations or groupings, experience that most complex of phenomena – politics. Change and the prospect of change are the most potent and obvious engines of politics. Change often brings to the surface tensions and potentialities for conflict that in quieter times remain dormant (Lacey 1977). However, as Ball (1987) reminds us, the argument can run another way and change can be the fruit and consequence of tension and conflict within and beyond the system. Whichever way we look at it, it is clear that change and politics will be found together. Mainstream political science accepts that opposition and resistance exist to some degree in all societies and organizations and that systems vary a great deal in the barriers or opportunities they present for the organization and expression of preferences and thus the opportunities for resistance, opposition and participation (Dahl 1973, McLennan 1973).

My focus in this chapter is the psychodynamic dimension of human engagement and change processes, which involve the familiar political patterns of grouping, splitting into factions, coalescing around differing ideas, perceptions and ideologies and alliances for and against individuals and groups and what they are perceived to stand for. There is also of course the dynamics of simple self-interest and ambition. Blase and Anderson (1995) take as their starting point in the study of the micro-politics of educational leadership the basic tenet of political science, 'that power is exercised when A gets B to do what B would otherwise not do'. Other theories of power and its use in organizations have been developed in recent years (Bachrach and Baratz 1962, Lukes 1974, Foucault 1977, Rappaport 1984), and of course the study of power and its use and distribution has been the subject of study from Plato and Aristotle onwards. My theory of micro-politics combines orthodox approaches from mainstream political science and the study of micro-politics in educational settings with definitions of reality deriving from the traditions of dynamical systems theory, psychiatry and organizational psychodynamics. The micro-political and psychodynamic elements are seen in a way as 'noise' in the system and like noise in physical deterministic systems they may lead to turbulent phenomena. These 'political' forces are what give deep complexity to organizations.

In this chapter I will restate briefly three sets of theory I developed in Chapter 3, which will act as the explanatory frame for understanding the micro-political issues covered here. These are, first, work based upon Bion's (1961) ideas on 'basic assumption' and 'work group' behaviour in groups; second, Argyris and Schon's (1978) work on models of learning in groups; and, third, the concept of system control parameters developed in complexity theory for physical deterministic systems (Gleick 1988, Briggs and Peat 1989, Stewart 1989) with many applications in the field of human organizations (Baumol and Benhabib 1989, Gemmell and Smith 1985, Zimmerman 1992, Stacey 1991, 1996, Goldstein 1994, Peters 1991, Wheatley 1992, Richardson 1991, Nonaka 1988). I will then proceed to describe a number of aspects of the political dimension and life at Edwardes College. These practical aspects of the micro-politics of change will be discussed in the context of: first, the politics of change, second, resistance to change and, third, learning in new ways. Finally I will draw together the discussion into the theoretical frame outlined above as both an explanatory/descriptive aid and an operational tool.

There is an important tradition of research and writing on the micro-politics of schools whose most significant recent work is Stephen Ball's (1987) *The Micro-politics of the School*. After a lengthy period of stagnation in the field of the sociology of school organization, he produced a work of real importance for schools in their complex day-to-day realities. Other work has focused on governance, leadership, power and conflict (Blase and Blase 1997), the politics of teachers' workplace and teachers' stress (Ozga 1988), teachers' resistance and deviance as well as language, discourse and power (Davies 1994). Much of this work deals with the normative, conscious and orthodox political realities of schools, but at the same time acknowledges the complex and unpredictable nature of schools as social organizations in *real* situations. Davies (1994: 3) for example states it exactly: 'One of the attractions, even temptations, of theories such as education management theories, is the urge to simplify, to find some single elegant crystalline way of explaining and predicting organizational life.'

I am aware of the pitfall Thomas Huxley expressed when he spoke of 'a beautiful theory killed by a nasty ugly little fact', and I hope to live with the messy and 'ugly little facts' of the realities of real-world educational situations.

In contrast to the tradition of study of the micro-politics and sociology of the school outlined above, I will be concentrating especially on the psychological and unconscious or semi-conscious forces that frequently affect individual and group behaviour. Although, of course, not all politics is unconscious, I take the view that individuals and groups do not always behave in ways that are explicable in terms of their rational and overt intentions. Jealousies, guilt, anxiety and undisclosed and often unrecognized struggles for power have a profound effect on the acceptance or rejection of rational solutions to apparently straightforward problems. We have seen in Chapter 2 that Bion (1991) suggests that in all situations of group interaction there will be simultaneously both a legitimate and a formal task, the primary task or *work group*, and another, deeper level of interaction referred to as the *basic assumption group* (Chapter 3). Bion observed that when the emotional atmosphere is at a low background level, it can assist the work of the group in performing its task. However, if basic assumption behaviour comes to dominate the behaviour of the group the task will become almost impossible. Instead, the group will act as if it has formed solely to perform an emotional task: to become dependent, to fight or to take flight from the task (or each other) or to rely on pairing within its members to find a solution or to fuse with each other (Turquet 1974). Basic assumption behaviours are adopted without any conscious intention on the part of the individuals concerned. They are unconscious group processes and lead people to 'regress' to psychotic and primitive forms of behaviour.

Bion developed his theory from earlier work by Klein (1975a, 1975b), and this led to decades of work at the Tavistock Institute in London (Miller and Rice 1967, Winnicott 1971, Miller 1983, 1989). Similar work was done at the A.K. Rice Institute in the USA (Gibbard, Hartmann and Mann 1974, Colman and Bexton 1975, Colman and Giller 1985).

My hypothesis is that occupation of the creative state requires a move away from too stable and fixed group behaviours but the avoidance of overwhelming basic assumption behaviour. In very rigid and fixed systems, basic assumption behaviour is often minimal; the faint emotion that can perhaps be detected is boredom or frustration. Group behaviour tends towards a static and fixed state, and control parameters such as connectivity, information flow and anxiety levels are low. Group learning is at a minimum; stability is at a maximum. By reference to my second theoretical frame, this is referred to as Learning Model I (Argyris and Schon 1978). The opposite of this is predominant basic assumption behaviour, which is, as we have seen, an equally unsatisfactory state of psychotic behaviours leading to anarchy and disintegration where performance of task is impossible. Here all rules and structure are loosened and become ineffective. Hierarchy, order and bureaucracy tend to break down. This is referred to as Learning Opposite Model I. When group members occupy Learning Model I and the stable frozen zone, they are frequently frustrated and cannot easily learn. In this situation there can be a tendency to switch to the Opposite Model I, which leads to highly unstable behaviour (Argyris and Schon 1978, Argyris 1999, Cohen, March and Olsen 1972).

What we were searching for at Edwardes College and UTS was the elusive space between the stable zone (Model I) and the unstable zone

(Opposite Model I); in other words, a 'phase transition' between the static state and group disintegration – rigidity and turbulence, work group and basic assumption behaviour. In this transitional state, basic assumption behaviour is present but in the background and contributes to learning without killing it. In the terms of Argyris and Schon, Learning Model II allows for deep double-loop learning and creativity. This transition between stable and unstable zones is a place of paradox as we have seen (Chapter 3, Table 3.1). In this state members of groups are able to play with ideas, they are able to use their imaginations to develop all sorts of possibilities for future action, new ways of doing things, new rituals and guiding values – the very stuff of politics. Above all, the group holds and allows for anxiety and manages it by caring and communicating.

As leadership and followership play an important role in this story and are similarly the stuff of politics, it will be helpful to say a few words on the psychodynamic theory of this. In the mature individual, the ego – that is, the concept of the self as a unique individual – mediates the relationships between the internal world of good and bad objects and the external world of reality, and this takes a 'leadership' role in relation to the personality. A central idea of psychoanalysis is that love and hate can be felt for the same person, especially in early infancy, and how this is managed and reconciled in the maturing process influences much of personality development in later life (Klein 1975a, 1975b). This fact of love and hate is intensified in the relations between leaders and followers. Followers depend on their leaders to identify a goal, identify ways of reaching it and lead towards it; a leader who fails or falters deprives his or her followers of satisfaction and may earn their hatred. This powerful mutual dependence increases the need for leaders and followers to defend themselves against the destructive power of their potential hostility. This, then, is another dimension, often hidden and unconscious, that plays a part in the game and process of the politics of change.

There is also a considerable literature on the more orthodox aspects of the politics and practice of leadership in schools (for instance Blase and Anderson 1995, Ball 1987, Maxcy 1991, Blase 1991, Hofstede 1994). Ball develops a classic politics of leadership with five style types in the performance of head teachers: *interpersonal, managerial, political, adversarial and authoritarian*. Blase and Anderson (1995) develop a micro-political leadership matrix with four similar leadership styles: *adversarial, democratic/empowering, facilitative and authoritarian*. Useful though these analyses are, I will be concentrating more on the psychodynamic and dynamical systems aspects of leadership and followership and organizational states.

What I have to say in this context of 'politics' and psychodynamics will, I hope, help to illuminate and explain why and how the college resisted and attempted to avoid moving into and occupying the space for creativity. I hope also to describe how the college did attempt to occupy the learning zone, and I will review the competing forces that were encountered in the process. This set of forces and ideas that underlie this dimension of the shadow and legitimate systems and their opposing currents are the unifying theme of what I will explore in this chapter.

If we analyse precisely what these forces and phenomena are, we will perhaps see that 'political' activity has its roots in the basic assumption archetypal drives within any group as well as in the opposite defensive behaviours of work group behaviour as described by Bion (1991) and the struggle between the two. Alongside these theories of organizational and group psychology, I will be setting out the theory of system control parameters mentioned above and will attempt to map the realities of the processes of change and learning at Edwardes College onto the five system control parameter values (outlined initially in Chapter 3): *levels and quality of information flow, connectivity among individuals and groups, varieties of behavioural schemas, power differentials and levels of anxiety and their containment.*

Throughout we will need to remind ourselves of the basic fact that change in an organization is almost certain to elicit resistance, turbulence and dissonance or what I have called 'noise'. The change agenda that we adopted touched upon structures, working practices and institutional culture. This would inevitably affect the interests and concerns of members of the community. Ball (1987) points out that 'Innovations are rarely neutral. They tend to advance or enhance the position of certain groups and disadvantage or damage the position of others.' Clearly identities and vested interests, self-concepts and long-established habits are challenged by change. It is therefore not surprising, as I shall demonstrate in the Edwardes College context, that change in educational institutions brings with it conflict between pro-change and resistance groups.

The politics of change at Edwardes College

In this chapter I will describe and reflect upon the political realities and forces that manifested themselves at Edwardes College as we moved forward into the change programme and as those changes began to take root in our practice and in the very thinking of the college. In broad outline the various stages of our development programme for the college followed the path outlined below:

1   First were the early days when attempts were made to test me, as the new principal, and the college by a small group of senior staff led by one or two powerful senior individuals. This was clearly a stage at which we were getting acquainted with one another. However, it seemed that one group in particular wished to exert their influence. It is possible that they saw a way to assert influence and power by causing difficulties for a new and apparently vulnerable principal. It is likely that the college as a community was experiencing basic assumption

behaviour of dependency on this group. They held considerable sway over many staff and became a focal point for resistance to change.

2   The second phase was the crucial stage when resistance lessened and early uncertainties diminished. In this stage basic assumption behaviour decreased and the emotional atmosphere became moderated, though 'explosions' did occur from time to time. By this stage I felt the staff could be categorized in three groups. The categorization of teachers has been the subject of a number of studies in recent years. Troman (2000) considers the reactions and relationships of teachers under stress in the face of the new managerialism, and government inter-vention in schools in the United Kingdom. He examines the issue of trust relations and categorizes a range of responses to the pressures of change. Other work, in the field of categories of teacher responses to change, includes Ball (1987), Ozga (1988) and Mac an Ghaill (1992). My three groups were: *Group X* (resisters of change), *Group Y* (neutral, observers) and *Group Z* (supporters, energizers, positive, learners).

It seemed that my task was to create a strong momentum towards Group Z and to try to present Group X from influencing others in the opposite direction. The tensions in both directions were strong.

3   In the next phase, changes began to flow. There began to be a sense of forward motion. More and more staff members began to support the new directions but at the same time small groups formed to resist change. Model II theory-in-use behaviours (Argyris 1999) were begin-ning to emerge, with real signs of creativity among some staff and a willingness to experiment, try new things and live with uncertainties.

4   Gradually the new culture of change was accepted and became the dominant reality, but still there was resistance. New structures and man-agement posts were filled by the able and the energetic, and not purely on a basis of seniority. This was perhaps the most culturally difficult and controversial innovation of all. It ran counter to the powerful local cultural norm of the primacy of the principle of seniority. Hierarchy and deference to seniors, irrespective of their abilities or qualities, is a universally respected norm. This is enshrined in the national pay scales for workers in government service, which are rigidly hierarchical. My decision to break with some of these norms in order to get good people into important management positions was arguably the riskiest move I made.

5   The fifth stage can perhaps be characterized as a stage when forces of resistance to change began to coalesce powerfully, mainly outside the institution among college alumni and elements in the provincial govern-ment. This stage melded into the time of preparations for the college's

centenary celebrations, which represented a very high-profile event. There were powerful elements which wanted to be associated with or have a controlling hand in this event. This was a time of exceptional turbulence in and around the college. It also coincided with the military coup of October 1999, in which the Nawaz Sharif government was toppled, and the instability of its aftermath. We wanted to present the college as a modern, effective and high-quality institution fit and ready to embark upon its second hundred years. The centenary was a good opportunity to bring all stakeholders and friends together to create a renewed commitment to and a new understanding of what the college stood for. At this stage other agendas and forces were coming forcefully into play and the shadow or recessive system became a much more potent and dangerous phenomenon.

These broad, impressionistic descriptions of our political journey are set within the context of the realities and problems of governance in the culture of Pakistan. If that nation has experienced one central problem, it has surely been the issue of governance. From the highest reaches of government down to fairly humble institutions there have been misuses in this area. There is frequently a failure and an unwillingness to understand the important distinction between governance and management – though, needless to say, this problem is by no means confined solely to Pakistan.

Resistance

Important work on teacher resistance and deviance has been done by Lynn Davies (1990, 1992, 1994), who portrays the realities of life in schools and not some anodyne, idealized, managerialist version of school life. Hofstede (1994) takes the case of a school in Switzerland where attempted reform led first to rebellion and then to naked repression on the part of the management, thus providing a vivid illustration of the resistance that can develop to changes in the power relationship within the institution and the wider culture. I was aware, especially at later stages in the improvement programme, that patterns of resistance were gradually developing at Edwardes College and in its wider cultural environment, though repression was not an option for action. I will describe below some of the ways this resistance manifested itself.

Staff professional development sessions at Edwardes College were mainly purposeful, orderly and constructive. As I show in Chapter 5, there was a tendency for them to be more formal than I wished, and I took steps to break up the formal patterns and shapes in order to allow for new ways of interacting and learning. I wanted above all to avoid replicating the classroom mode of passive learning. I wanted to encourage real engagement and real learning of new attitudes, behaviours and understandings. This would constitute an increase in levels of control parameter values of *connectivity and information flow*.

Naturally there were those who hung back or were sceptical. Gradually they were able to be won over, and it was exciting to see how many of them began to engage after their initial passivity. There was another group who were hostile or negative, though seldom openly. Action in the shadow system is often covert. Due to the dominant culture of deference to seniority, this negativity lay very hidden for much of the time but was nevertheless a very real force. As principal I had to work hard to hear some of these negative voices and interpret how they were impacting upon other groups among the staff. Often I relied upon trusted staff members to relay information on shadow-system activity. One also has to use one's intuition.

Beginning to learn in new ways

There came a time when early resistance waned and the power of what I have called Group X – the determined resisters of change – was largely neutralized. One notable exception was that of a strong supporter of change, an important member of the SMT, suddenly switching 'allegiance' and reverting to Group X. On the other hand, there was a steady movement of non-committed members from Group Y who shifted more towards Group Z, which gradually came to hold the dominant position and wield the main influence.

A number of new staff members were appointed and immediately had a positive impact on Group Z, bringing considerable freshness, energy and openness to new ways. I invested heavily in these new staff by holding weekly meetings at which they were able to discuss a range of professional matters. Other members of staff who had joined in the previous three years were also invited to attend. These sessions were sometimes led by me, but more often by a senior member of staff. They were used as a means of communicating and informing younger staff about routine practices and procedures as well as for discussing policies and current debates; at other times, for training and professional development in a wider sense. Some of the most creative and interesting sessions were in the form of micro teaching workshops. One new staff member would prepare a short instructional session of about fifteen minutes and this was followed by a group discussion and critique on the mini-lesson. These weekly gatherings represented a deliberate increase in the levels of *connectivity and information*. They provided a new channel of communication and interaction allowing younger staff to work together around a positive agenda aimed at helping them in their professional lives as well as enhancing quality issues in the college. I stepped back as much as possible, allowing other senior staff to run the sessions wherever possible.

Almost every major change that was introduced was greeted with scepticism. My diary records such comments as: '*It couldn't work here.*', '*This is not our way.'* and *'It's too much work.'* In one instance when I requested that staff place roll numbers on all desks during exams to identify students, an SMT member reported to me that some staff were refusing to comply and were saying, *'The principal is treating us like clerks.'* I regarded this procedure as being of such importance in combating cheating that I went into the exam hall along with one or two SMT members and we started to do the work ourselves. Immediately the staff came in and stopped us, and without further complaint completed the work in a matter of minutes. Of course, in the culture of Peshawar, it would have been usual for a servant to do the work, but I felt it should be done by academic staff. However, in almost every case the complaints did not last long and the innovation worked well; comments became positive and there was a sense of rising professional self-esteem. Gradually I began to feel that most staff members were becoming more positive and engaged, but also that those elements who still hung back (Group Y) or strongly opposed (Group X) were increasingly being outflanked and neutralized by a surge of positive support from parents and students. There is an extensive literature on the role of parents and students in relation to teachers indicating that parental influence can be either supportive or negative and that the key issues around which interactions occur are academic instruction and discipline (for example Blase 1991, Ball 1987, Blase and Anderson 1995).

By the end of the second year, major changes had been achieved and were beginning to be well received and appreciated. These included:

- New assessment and reporting procedures (*information*)
- Greatly increased contact with parents (*information and connectivity*)
- New management structures for academic and pastoral management (*power differentials, anxiety containment, variety*)
- A new timetable
- A new referral system and devolved disciplinary procedures (*information, power differentials, variety*)
- Regular and systematic professional development (*information, connectivity, variety*).

(Where appropriate relevant control parameters are given in parentheses.)

As a result students, parents and staff became better informed. Regular support and care were available through tutors and pastoral teams. Falsification and inaccuracy in attendance and assessment figures were much reduced. There was a great deal of positive comment and feedback from the community. This came in a variety of ways: through parents verbally or by letter, from people in the community and via members of staff who relayed some of the opinion they picked up. In a number of important ways the five control parameters of the system were changing. There were increased levels of *information* and *connectivity*. This fed through into increased levels of *anxiety* and *variety of behaviour*. The delegation of roles and responsibilities was leading to lower levels of *power differentials* within the system.

I suggest that changes had occurred in the control parameter values of the system which were beginning to allow creativity to emerge. Group Z, perceived to be 'led' by me,[1] the principal, and centred on the Senior Management Team (SMT), was beginning to attempt to occupy the 'space for creativity', and Group X was resisting that process.

The five system control parameter values – *a) quality and rate of flow of information, b) richness of connectivity, c) degree of variety of schemas, d) power differentials and e) level of contained anxiety* – were changing. The quantity and availability of accurate and useful *information* in the college had increased markedly. Levels had been extremely low at the start of the change programme. It was not long before staff knew much more about students' academic and pastoral situations as well as about college policies and practices. *Richness of connectivity* was variable, but over time had settled more towards the mean required for effective system learning. There was a much higher incidence of staff engaging in professional discussions of all sorts, both in the legitimate and in the recessive or shadow system. *Variety of schemas* was growing from a low base as some staff gained the confidence to try new ways of doing things both in the classroom and out. In some cases new posts and roles required new behaviours. In the case of the tutorial system, all staff had a new role requiring very new forms of classroom behaviour. For many of them it was a new experience to spend time with students outside the normal task of teaching a given subject. Instead they had to learn new behaviours concerned with the delivery of pastoral care, academic support and exploring often sensitive issues raised through the embryonic pastoral curriculum. There was a time when all students were attending AIDS awareness lectures given by members of an NGO working in the field of HIV/AIDS, and these sessions were followed up in tutorial groups. Some staff were able to respond well with interesting ways of engaging the students; others were unable to cope and reverted to defensive traditional behaviours, for example getting students to sit and catch up with classwork. *Power differentials* were being reduced from the very high levels of the traditional rigid hierarchy as I delegated responsibility and created new management structures. *Levels of contained anxiety* were oscillating but in an upward curve. Changes, new roles and new behaviours were bound to lead to increases in anxiety. Real creativity and double-loop learning would depend upon modulating these variables into critical or optimum levels.

Features of the system at this stage included the following elements:

- New management structures and procedures introduced and progressively modified.
- New practices, attitudes and behaviours were beginning to appear. There was an increased variety of behavioural schemas and an increased

willingness to try new behaviours. For example, some members of staff were willing to experiment with mutually agreed pairings for the purpose of observing each other's classroom practice and supporting each other. This was a risky undertaking in a context and culture where set and traditional behaviours were dominant and where conformity was strong. Some staff members were willing to come forward with new ideas and to present them either to me or, on occasion, at the SMT meetings at my invitation.

• Fluctuating but increased anxiety. Anxiety was contained through reassurance, meetings, briefings, counselling and coaching. On several occasions staff with important jobs came to me to say that they wished to resign from their responsible positions because they could not handle the pressure (mainly from colleagues). In every case, after counselling and encouragement by me, they continued with great success. However, in some cases the expressed wish to resign was repeated more than once. One such individual said he felt unable to continue because of the pressure and bitterness from certain other staff members (Group X). There were occasions when I felt the pressure on all of us was getting to be too great and tried to slow the pace of change. This was an overt and conscious act of modulation of one of the key system parameter values: *anxiety*. I recognized that anxiety was bound to be experienced by all of us and must be allowed but managed through a process of collegiality and sharing of concerns, but that it could become a negative factor if not moderated.

• Increased collaboration and collegiality. Hargreaves (1991) discusses collegiality – contrived and otherwise – and considers various definitions and meanings of collegiality. Increases in teamwork and collegiality helped to contain anxiety. Many staff members in Group Z gave each other good support. Some members of Group Z were proactive in counselling non-committed individuals in Group Y, with some very positive results. Several members of the management group reported to me on their engagements with other selected members of staff who we felt needed encouragement. The activity of these members of the management team was very mature and creative. They headed off trouble on occasion by quietly counselling others. They acted as an important channel of communication and connectivity to ensure that others knew what was *really* intended. This often amounted to going beyond the overt, surface levels of the change, which were usually well understood, and explaining that there was no hidden or sinister agenda which was sometimes imagined or propagated by Group X leaders – in effect, a quiet exercise in winning hearts and minds. I also encouraged managers to build their own teams just as I was building the SMT. One senior member of the team complained at an SMT meeting that many tutors were not performing as well as he had hoped, and he took the familiar line of looking to the principal to solve his problem. I turned the matter discreetly back to him and to all in the room by saying that we all had to win over our teams, energizing and inspiring them to want to fulfil their roles creatively and energetically. The SMT members were gently being required to face up to the leadership aspects of their roles; this involved reduced *power differentials* from a centre–periphery perspective.

- The pro-change group (Group Z) was also beginning to play creatively in the shadow system with 'creative destruction' (Stacey 1996). Old methods and practices were questioned and began to be replaced. The initiative was coming, as often as not, from individuals and small groups in the SMT and even from departments. For example new ways of conducting exams, setting and marking papers, security for papers and new methods of timetabling were tried, modified and tried again. New courses and approaches came from one department. What did not work was changed, and what worked was developed in a cycle of 'creative destruction'. On the other hand, the resistance group (Group X) defended the status quo and felt threatened.

- *Power differentials* were reduced and the distribution of influence and decision-making became wider and more fluid. The principal was still held in high respect as the culture demanded, but the aim was still very much to devolve responsibility and influence and to allow staff to show initiative. Staff members exercised new responsibilities and new formal structures were put in place to legitimize these new management and influencing roles. Central decision-making became more consultative. Heads of department were encouraged to lead their teams and to take responsibility for the performance of their teams.

The above changes seemed to signal a gradual change of the dominant 'theory-in-use' that dominated the basic assumptions and psychodynamics of the college, but there remained a hard core of resistance among those who held to the existing 'theory-in-use'. As we will see, the existing 'theory of its own purpose' is along the lines of: 'We are a family, and the college is here to provide us with security and lifelong employment. We are here to provide education in the narrow traditional sense. Seniority is the prime determinant of power and influence and respect.' The new 'theory of its own purpose' seemed to say: 'We can and we must develop and learn by adopting new styles and practices and structures. The world is changing and we must change too. We can achieve excellence through innovation, effort and creativity. Influence goes to those who are committed and capable of change.' The new state of the college was exhibiting control parameter values that were moving closer to the optimal values for occupying the space for creativity phase transition.

This period of increasing turbulence coincided, as we have seen, with greatly increased instability in the wider political environment. The Nawaz Sharif regime was toppled by a military coup after a period of increasing uncertainty. Three different provincial governors came and went within less than a year, and at one point I had had three chairmen in the space of three months. At the same time provincial government secretaries – members of the board – came and went, giving the feeling of shifting sands. With the Bishop absent for two years on an appointment in London, I found that the college board had changed almost entirely during less than a year: out of a board of twelve members over half were completely new and unfamiliar with the college and almost no one was really familiar with the background to the current situation.

A key feature of dynamical systems theory is the nature of the interaction between a system and its environment. In the year of the college centenary a number of important developments coincided. First, the system parameters in the college were rising as we pushed forward with the change programme. All seemed to be well on this front, and the atmosphere was most encouraging, with a lot of excellent work taking place: the 1999 examination results were the best for at least thirty years. Second, because we were in the centenary year it became clear that different interest groups saw this as an opportunity to take a high profile for their own purposes. Third, the general political and cultural environment was undergoing profound, disturbing and even threatening changes. This combination of forces made 'navigation' difficult.

States of the control parameters at different system states

I have attempted to show in this chapter that as a change programme progresses, so the five control parameters of the system undergo change. I have also attempted to show how these changes are often related to activity in the shadow system and to levels of *basic assumption* behaviour and, its opposite, *work group* or *defensive* behaviour. I have described the micro-politics at Edwardes College and developed a descriptive theory of what I witnessed happening. I have also suggested that what pushes an organization from the stable state into the creative zone or into radical instability and chaos are the five control parameters: *rate of information flow, degree of diversity, richness of connectivity, degree of power differentials and level of contained anxiety*. The relationship of the five control parameters to the state of the system as a whole is depicted in Table 4.1.

The central column or creative state in Table 4.1 represents a zone of paradox as described in Chapter 3. In the creative state it is likely that the following mix of paradoxical conditions listed on p. 49 will be found.

In the terms of Table 4.1, other features can be mapped. One example is the relation of models of group learning (Argyris and Schon 1978, Argyris 1999) referred to in Chapter 3. Rigid system states are associated with Model I learning. Creative system states are associated with Model II learning. Chaotic system states are associated with Opposite Model I learning.

Another mapping relevant to system states is the operation of *basic assumption* behaviour and *work group* behaviour (Bion 1961). Rigid system states are associated with dominant *work group* and *defensive* behaviour. Chaotic states are associated with dominant *basic assumption* behaviour. Creative system states are associated with a constructive mix of *work group* and *basic assumption* behaviour in such proportions that the emotional content and atmosphere provided by *basic assumption* behaviour contribute powerfully and creatively to task performance and single- and double-loop learning without flipping over into neurotic and psychotic behaviours. These combinations and associations of system states, learning models and behaviour types are brought together and illustrated in Table 4.2.

Naturally, in reality the distinctions between the rigid, creative and chaotic zones are very fluid. One state shades in subtle nuances into another. Each of the five control parameters is interconnected with the others so that they affect one another in ever-changing patterns from which the state of the system emerges. In terms of the five stages of development of the micro-political processes at Edwardes College outlined above we can see that the stages relate to the system states and control parameters roughly as follows:

Stages 1–2: Rigid   Control parameter values at the start of the programme are low. The system is in a static and stable state. There is a low level of information and such information as is available is poor quality and not used effectively in the proper forums. For example, teachers and tutors do not have good information on academic and pastoral matters. There is strong resistance to change centred on Group X. The new principal is being tested.

Stage 3: Less rigid   In this stage, control parameters are moving slightly towards optimal values. Resistance to change and innovation are still strong, especially among some older and more senior staff. There is uncertainty among some staff members about new directions and how they will cope.

Stage 4: Creative   At this stage the new culture of change is becoming established, accepted and appreciated. New management roles and processes are accepted and begin to have positive effects on student outcomes. Rigid ideas on seniority seem to soften as new post holders become established. Power and influence becomes more dispersed through the controlled delegation of authority; collaboration, teamwork and collegiality increase. There is further movement towards optimal levels of control parameter values. *Power differentials* are declining. *Anxiety* is contained. *Information, connectivity and variety* are on the increase. By this stage levels of control parameters are at their best as the college moves haltingly towards effective learning and innovation. For cultural reasons *power differentials* remain

Table 4.1 States of control parameters at the three states of the organization

	Rigid	Creative	Chaotic
Information flow	Low-level flow of information Information on 'need to know' basis Centralized information control Culture of secrecy Information retained in formal channels and systems	Information flows more freely through system Information spills out of formal systems, grapevine becomes active Information reaches local forums and is acted upon in creative ways Redundant information is removed	Information overload Information of all types (reliable and unreliable) freely available Too much information causes stress and unnecessary aggravation Great stress on both legitimate and shadow systems, tipping them into chaos
Connectivity	Staff isolated, mind own business Get on with job, retreat into privacy of classroom Tradition and conformity dominate Few but strong affective personal ties Interactions mainly in formal settings	Rich – but not too rich – discourse and engagement Members creatively engaged with each other Caring culture, able to handle personal and professional crises Many firm affective personal ties	Intrigue and petty politicking rife Large no. of connections and personal ties, both weak and strong Discourse is conspiratorial and factional with high emotional tone Rumours abound, hyperactive grapevine

Variety of schemas	Conformity and uniformity of practice often based on traditional orthodoxies. Eccentricity is resisted	Rich variety of action and behaviour. Experimental behaviour encouraged as well as tempered. Old methods, values and styles questioned, tested and sometimes replaced. More eccentricity accepted	Anything goes culture. Highly eccentric and endlessly diversified behaviours. Little conformity or perceived order. Sense of anarchy and confusion
Power differentials	High power differentials. Steep and rigid hierarchies, fixed elite wields most power. Strong central control, forceful oppressive authority. Shadow system driven underground. Atmosphere of fear	Combination of clear management structure and freedom to express opinions and creativity. Clear delegation and appropriate dispersal of power. Team-building, consultation and collegiality	Power widely dispersed, nobody in control. Power vacuum, anarchic conditions. Nobody takes decisions. Weak legitimate system, few clear rules, little deference
Anxiety levels	Apparent levels of anxiety low. Low levels of worry about work. Anxiety contained and avoided by bureaucratic norms and structures	Anxiety is experienced and held and contained in 'good enough manner'. Effective holding of anxiety is provided by members themselves. Holding is good enough if there is mutual trust and liking. Counselling, coaching and support in teams is available to all	High level of anxiety and uncertainty. No counselling, coaching or support. Atmosphere of rule of the jungle. Emotional and neurotic tone to interactions

Table 4.2 Learning models, behaviour patterns and shadow system in the three system states

	Rigid	Creative	Chaotic
Learning model (theory-in-use)	Model I	Model II	Opposite Model I
Basic assumption behaviour	Low	Moderated	Dominant
Work group behaviour	Dominant	Moderated	Low
Shadow system	Quiescent	Active–creative	Active–subversive

high, though less so than in the early stages. *Variety of schemas* remains relatively low, reflecting a reluctance to change habits and patterns of professional activity, especially in the classroom. There was never a time when the system as a whole reached the phase transition creative zone or truly optimal levels. However, there was a time when some groups were manifesting powerful learning and creativity in specific areas, while others were very much stuck in the rigid, static state.

Stage 5: Elements of chaos　This stage is dominated by struggles in the board of governors, tensions in the Christian community, a reactivation of the staff association and increased activity in Group X and among powerful outsiders. This is set in the context of a wider environment that is undergoing great political turbulence (see above). External turbulence begins to affect the state of the college. Micro-political tensions and difficulties begin to impact upon the atmosphere of the college. Levels of *anxiety* rise sharply along with *connectivity*, both of which move towards levels above the optimum. At this stage the turbulence of the wider cultural and political environment, combined with internal resistance in the shadow system, forced some of the control parameter values above optimal levels. It is likely that the system would have returned to a more stable state if the improvement programme had continued beyond the exceptional circumstances of the centenary. With a new term and year, events would undoubtedly have settled down and normal routines would have been restored after the high excitement of the centenary and all the political manoeuvrings.

　　Much further research is of course needed into precise audits and measures of specific details of practice, procedure and structure in schools and colleges that contribute to the various system control parameters.

　　A great deal of what I have described here concerning system states and control parameters can be mapped and transposed onto other dimensions of complex dynamical systems whether these are the paradoxical states and contrasts between Model I, Model II and Opposite Model I behaviours, or details of neurotic and defensive behaviours or features of complex adaptive systems. All these qualities and system control parameters can be mapped in relation to the phase transition zone that complexity science identifies as a key feature of all complex dynamical systems and of which in human systems we know all too little at this time.

The theoretical understanding of organizations expressed in this chapter and in the theoretical framework developed in Chapters 2 and 3 has important consequences for our understanding of management strategies in schools and colleges. The existing dominant framework with its central question, *How can we manage and design our schools to yield successful outcomes?*, can give way to different questions and a different dominant framework. The linear equilibrium modes can give way to a non-linear approach where we seek to modulate the control parameters to push the organization into – but not beyond – the zone for creativity. Our 'intentionality' is therefore shifted away from a primary focus on inputs and outcomes to a concern for states of the organization out of which fitness for purpose can grow. In place of the dominance of interventionist and mechanistic methods, we can frame a new central question: *How can we understand and make sense of our schools and their unpredictable nature? How can we cultivate autopoietic (self-referential) system states that generate powerful creativity and learning, which at the same time acknowledge their complex and unpredictable nature and allow for self-organization?*

In the context of much psychological research (Bion 1961, Argyris and Schon 1978) the key control parameter used for moving groups between the stable and unstable zones of behaviour and into the creative zone is the level of the group's anxiety. In the words of Stacey (1996: 150–151),

Anxiety is tuned up by removing containing structures, such as Learning Model I behaviour or conventional leadership. The Group can be returned to the stable zone by re-erecting the containing structures and thus reducing the levels of anxiety. However, when anxiety is at an intermediate level, at some critical point enough challenge and contention exist to provoke group members into some form of exploration, but also enough emotional containment of that anxiety to prevent them from being submerged by basic assumption behaviour. At critical points of anxiety containment, groups of people can work and perform double-loop learning, avoiding both the 'psychotic fantasy' of the unstable zone and the rigidly 'defensive behaviours' of the stable zone.

Note

1 It should be emphasized that although I led the SMT and the college, I did not see myself as leading any particular group. My role was to lead all disinterestedly. Therefore my so-called 'leadership' of Group Z was only a by-product of the change agenda and not an intended identifier.

5 Deep learning and Professional Development in the learning organization

Professional Development (PD) is widely accepted as a central feature of any improvement strategy and can perhaps be seen as the very heart of attempts to create a learning culture. Indeed, PD is an important element capable of enhancing what I have referred to as 'system cognition'. If we are to take the learning organization seriously, then professional learning must be central. It is, therefore, conceptualized not as an isolated or individual or external activity but as a collective or collegial process built into the very fabric or 'cognitive system' of the institution. The aim of professional development in a learning organization is to encourage 'technical' professional practice as well as what I have described above (see Chapter 3) as 'double-loop' learning in which behaviour is changed through questioning institutional, group and individual schemas and modifying them through processes of replication and mutation. I will show in this chapter how professional development activity can be an important instrument in modifying all the key system control parameters (as discussed in Chapters 3 and 4) to move into the creative state phase transition. It is also the area in which Model I behaviours are discouraged and Model II behaviours developed so that deep creativity and learning grow.

Thinking about professional development has been profoundly influenced in recent decades by the study of organizational behaviour. Developments in this field have included the well-known classical human needs theories of Maslow (1954) and Alderfer (1972); the theories of human nature of McGregor (1960); Rogers' (1967) practical development of the ideas of Maslow; the theories of multiple intelligences developed by Handy (1990); the motivation theory of Herzberg (1966) and Handy (1976); and the life-cycle theory of Erikson (1977).

Underpinning all these studies and schools of thought in organizational behaviour is the 'given' that a school's staff is its most valuable and most costly asset and, therefore, staff development is central to institutional development. The literature of the past fifty years has consistently emphasized the importance of the individual and personhood so that personality, motivation, varieties of multiple intelligence, fulfilment of potential, life-cycle analysis and empowerment have each played an important role in the development of current thinking. There has always been, and probably always will be, a tension between an emphasis on organizational aims and personal aims in staff development. It seems sensible to seek a harmonious balance between the two.

Traditionally, professional development has been seen as controlled, planned and conducted in fairly formal settings and styles often employing predominantly top-down management methods and focusing mainly on knowledge and skills. In the last ten years professional development has increasingly moved away from these models to more school-based inter-active modes.

Basic elements in the design and implementation of Professional Development include the following:

1   The programme is largely school-based with the staff planning, design-ing and managing the bulk of the activities. The content is selected and designed to meet the needs of the staff as identified through a number of mechanisms such as systems of staff appraisal, departmental meetings and development plans, heads of department meetings, interviews and consultations. It is important that staff have a genuine stake in, and ownership of, their own professional development through the devolu-tion of control, content and design by gradual stages.
2   Professional development is variously designed around and initiated by individuals, groups and the whole institution.
3   Professional development activities should focus on objectives within the behavioural, affective and cognitive domains with a balanced enhance-ment of the following areas of professional knowledge and skills:
    a) Subject knowledge, techniques, teaching performance and teamwork
    b) Commitment, confidence, flexibility, satisfaction, trust in colleagues, positive school ethos and atmosphere
    c) Understanding of current educational best practice and trends, role clarification, skills in self-appraisal, understanding of institutional policies and mission, development of values and philosophy
4   Collaboration with a variety of external agencies and institutions with a view to establishing local professional development networks.

Traditional, linear approaches to professional development view the process as essentially a 'technical–rational' input into 'explicit' teacher expertise and knowledge. Our approach at Edwardes College and at UTS was aimed much more at developing discourses and reflective processes that would build what Fullan (1999) refers to as 'tacit' knowledge. While we were certainly aiming to develop best practice in many areas of our work at Edwardes College, I wanted to achieve something much more powerful. Best practices are not just discrete finished products; they are also develop-ing, changing processes and bodies of expertise. I wanted to create an environment which fostered the ability to generate new ideas and above all new behaviours, and generate them from within our own collective resources. This was going to be a complex and difficult process, and it would involve the risky process of allowing and incorporating new ideas and behaviours.

The focus, therefore, should be upon building and cultivating a culture of organizational learning and cognition where individual learning is woven into group and collective learning; where explicit 'technical' knowledge is systematically turned into implicit or tacit knowledge. This tacit knowledge is composed of skills, beliefs, ways of doing things, values and emotions. It may often be below the level of immediate consciousness – the shadow system referred to in Chapters 2 and 3 – while explicit knowledge is made up of words, statistics and formal data and information at a rational and conscious level. Much SEI research and practice has focused on the latter at the expense of the former. To avoid this means seeking to create an intricate, delicate and embedded culture of interaction within the school and its external relationships that can enable double-loop learning and real creativity. This can lead to what Nonaka and Tacheuchi (1995: 3) refer to as 'organizational knowledge'. 'By organizational knowledge creation we mean the capacity of a company as a whole to create new knowledge, disseminate it throughout the organization, and embody it in products, services and systems.'

Given this understanding, it is easy to see why the crude attempt to transfer individual school improvement strategies from one institution to another and to create blanket factorial approaches to school improvement yield such disappointing results. What cannot be transferred in this way are the tacit levels of knowledge needed for sustainable fitness and effectiveness.

Wheatley (1992: 7) states two powerful arguments for a reflexive approach to organizational learning on the grounds that the transfer of good practices is very difficult.

> First, I no longer believe that organizations can be changed by imposing a model developed elsewhere. So little transfers to, or even inspires, those trying to work at change in their own organizations. Second, and much more important, the new physics cogently explains that there is no objective reality out there waiting to reveal its secrets. There are no recipes or formulae, no checklists or advice that describe 'reality'. There is only what we create through our engagement with others and with events. Nothing really transfers; everything is always new and different and unique to each of us.

Fullan (1999: 63) makes a very similar point in the educational context.

> You should never worry about your good ideas being stolen in educational reform, because even when people are sincerely motivated to

learn from you, they have a devil of a time doing so. Transferability of ideas is a complex problem of the highest order.

Features of the Professional Development programme

Professional Development was placed in a central position at Edwardes College in order to make it a regular, ongoing feature of our working lives and to promote the culture of organizational learning described above. We aimed to tap both external resources as well as the rich internal resources of our own staff. I took as a central credo, in line with complexity thinking, that we are our own best resource with deep and rich veins of tacit and professional knowledge and potentiality, much of it lying deep and dormant.

The formal elements of the PD programme were as follows:

- Owned by the staff (*power differentials and connectivity*)
- Occasional full-day PD conferences for whole staff (*information, connectivity*)
- Occasional workshops for groups (*connectivity, variety*)
- Regular department-based PD activity (*information, connectivity, variety*)
- Management and leadership group development (*information, connectivity*)
- Visits and links to other institutions (*information, variety*)
- Encouragement of multiple informal, semi-formal and formal groups, discourses and quality circles, including professional pairings for mutual observation of classroom practice (*variety, connectivity, anxiety containment*)
- Use of staff and student questionnaires on conditions in the college and the quality of learning situations (*information*)
- College audit (*information*).

(Relevant control parameters are given in parentheses.)

The thematic thread and common approach in all these elements is the attempt to increase connectivity, professional communication and information flow in the search for deep organizational learning and new behaviours.

Regular professional engagement helps especially to increase the levels of two important system control parameters (discussed in Chapter 3): *rate of information flow* and the *degree of connectivity*. Also one of the outcomes of PD activity is to increase the levels of a third control parameter, *variety of schemas*, and indirectly to modify to some extent the fourth control parameter, *power differentials* in so far as the sessions involve all staff in discussion of matters of policy from which they are often excluded.

Institutional links and visits

Reaching out to external resources and communities is an important part of professional development. This is not in any sense because staffs are incapable of managing their own professional learning. Indeed, a systems approach to PD must build the idea that the members of a learning organization are the prime resource. There is no need constantly to seek 'experts' or gurus to solve problems. Above all, it is important not to replicate the model – so common in many parts of the world – where staff 'go out' and 'complete' a course, often of an academic and didactic type. It is important to cultivate a different model for professional learning. Fullan (1999: 18) expresses the model well when he says, 'Connection with the wider environment is critical for success (the best organizations learn externally as well as internally).' It is easy to make the mistake of working hard on your internal professional development while at the same time failing to be alert and proactive towards the external world, which is rich with resources and signposts. It is well accepted in the industrial and corporate world that successful, productive organizations import and absorb knowledge from outside.

Local linkages may include visits to local schools and colleges, some formal training opportunities provided by agencies and universities, local and national businesses and professional bodies. At Edwardes College, a very important element of our external linkages was the British Council-funded PD link with the University of Birmingham School of Education, which evolved further links and interactions with Birmingham City LEA and some individual institutions in the United Kingdom. This range of external engagements was a major increase on what had been the norm before.

The University of Birmingham was clearly a high-profile engagement, and it played a central part in much of our formal professional learning. Three or four Edwardes College staff visited Birmingham each year and two to three staff from Birmingham visited Edwardes College. Birmingham staff made contributions in a number of ways. They led formal full staff PD sessions and they consulted with departments, groups and individuals. On occasion formal advice was given to the principal and Senior Management Team (SMT) on administrative and management matters, and written reports were made on a number of aspects of college life. Equally important, visitors from Birmingham made warm friendships and in very large measure gained the confidence of Edwardes College staff.

On the Birmingham visits Edwardes College staff experienced a variety of placements in schools and colleges as well as visits to the Birmingham City local education authority school improvement centre in Harborne. They also spent time with staff in the School of Education and some other departments on various enrichment activities.

The main value of this exercise lay undoubtedly in the brief but powerful exposure to the very different professional cultures of English schools and colleges. Staff got to see a wide range of professional practice relevant to them and to experience a range of institutions with very individual problems and strengths. This model allows for and encourages some form of 'crossover replication' of behavioural schemas as a result of this exposure. In this way new varieties of behaviour can be learned, absorbed and adapted. This form of interconnection and interaction can lead to powerful 'communities of practice' and what Tim Brighouse, chief executive officer of Birmingham LEA, refers to as 'collegiate academies' – collections of schools working together on a range of initiatives. There is no doubt that some staff showed changes and improvements in aspects of their work as a result of such visits to Birmingham. For example, one group who visited that city came back with a range of management ideas and tools relating to their areas of responsibility: timetabling, the management of admissions, the management of examinations, and recording, analysing, displaying and acting upon examination results. Another group showed significant learning in the area of pastoral management and the pastoral curriculum.

Developing the key purpose statement and vision

This group work aimed to give staff a chance to discuss in depth certain aspects of the college and to try to look forward to the sorts of directions the college should seek to take. The discussions were structured around a handout that contained a number of activities to help keep the group focused. Each group was asked to submit a written statement on each of the following four elements contained in the structured worksheet:

1   Basic purpose (in no more than ten words)
2   Five items that will help achieve our purpose
3   Five items that will hinder our purpose
4   Full key purpose or 'quality' statement.

The notes attached to the worksheet stated that responses should be written in terms against which progress could be checked and that the final statement should point to a state that it would be desirable for the college to reach in four or five years. Some of the responses to the two key-purpose statements are outlined in Table 5.1.

The language of many of these responses is revealing of the mindset that was dominant at the college. When asked to consider purposes, staff found difficulty in making focused, practical suggestions. Instead, many of the responses took the broad, generalized forms given below, exhibiting a romanticized, somewhat idealized view of the college, for example: *'to keep the insignia of the college', 'apprise students of human values and ethics for betterment of society', 'polish personality, create future leaders and better human beings'*. This indicates a form of discourse and a

Table 5.1 Group responses to key purposes statements

Item	Group A	Group B	Group C	Group D
Basic purpose	To apprise students of human values and ethics for the betterment of society	Provide quality teaching, polish personality, create future leaders and better human beings	Learning through motivation, discipline and quality teaching	Impart quality education
Full key purpose	To adhere to the motto of our college, 'Ad majorem dei gloriam'	Nil	Mutual trust and high achievement	Provide exemplary teaching and take care of weaker students

language-in-use in the college set in a highly traditional mode. This style of response is partly attributable to the fact that these were issues that had not been discussed at all previously and staff seemed to have little frame of reference within which to think about future goals and purposes.

The most popular items that were to help achieve our purpose included the following:

- Clarity of vision
- Commitment
- Good pay
- Good teaching atmosphere
- A compassionate boss
- Good teachers, modern techniques of teaching
- Efficient administration
- Strict discipline
- High-quality students.

The items considered most likely to be a hindrance to our purpose included:

- Lack of recognition
- Lack of teamwork and trust
- Poor leadership
- Large class sizes and lack of classroom space
- Lack of incentives
- Financial constraints of the college
- Lack of cooperation from parents.

These responses showed a mixture of hard-headed pragmatism (as in class sizes, salary, financial constraint) and ill-defined idealism (as in creating moral and ethical values for the betterment of society).

The school culture and the shadow system

What I have described so far is primarily the formal, legitimate and normative procedures, practices and structures that were introduced or developed as part of our improvement programme. All these initiatives in and of themselves would not have led to deep and permanent changes. The really elusive – but at the same time desirable – aspect of professional development and institutional improvement is change to the culture and behavioural schemas of individuals and the organization. I have argued in Chapter 3 that real 'double-loop' institutional learning involves 'playing' in the 'recessive' or 'shadow' system, and this is where both deep and powerful learning and change can occur but at the same time where real dangers lie. Our understanding of the psychodynamics and realities of dynamical systems is crucial in this respect. Beneath and beyond the normative and legitimate systems that we established for individual and group professional learning (outlined above), we may begin to reach the hidden and shadow spaces and subtle points of engagement where deep institutional learning takes place. Perhaps this is a function of the way the leadership is able to set up the right resonance and the most favourable contexts for professional encounters. It is also a function of the ability of the organization to play in the shadow system without entering a destructive or chaotic mode in which basic assumption behaviour takes hold (see Chapter 3). Playing in the shadow means many things. It means opening up for discussion things that in a more rigid and defensive system would not be aired. It means allowing comment that may appear critical of the aims and agendas of those in authority. It means opening up for scrutiny power differentials and professional relationships. It means staff at all levels recognizing the need to exercise their leadership appropriately and the courage this may require. It means everyone seeing that they must shoulder some responsibility. It means allowing informal groups to form around new ideas and initiatives. It means allowing ways of doing things that may not be the norm within the existing bureaucratic structure. It means having the courage of one's convictions and standing up for what is professionally valuable and right. Above all, it means holding and living with *anxiety* and not avoiding it.

Allowing free play in the shadow system is potentially dangerous as it represents a large increase in *connectivity* and a growth in potentially political and destabilizing activity, and this was especially so in a rigidly hierarchical society like Peshawar and Edwardes College, which is ill-equipped to deal with such a situation. However, the central insight of dynamical systems and complexity theory is that complex adaptive systems are networks of agents which interact according to schemas that contain both dominant and recessive parts, and that these complex adaptive systems are creative only when they operate in what can be termed the space for novelty or the creative state. As I have argued above, this creative state is a far-from-equilibrium phase transition at the 'edge of chaos'. It is a state of paradoxes that is a mixture of stability and instability and is driven by the contradictory dynamics of competition and cooperation, amplification and constraint, anxiety and security, diversity and conformity. When the system operates in this zone it becomes radically unpredictable, and it evolves and changes through a process of creative destruction and reconstruction in which recessive schemas undermine dominant schemas to produce emergent outcomes and learning. We might say that formal didactic methods of teaching along with a traditional view of the college and its purposes had been dominant schemas, and that the search for more modern and interactive styles of teaching along with a radically different conception of the college and its purposes were new schemas attempting to undermine the old styles. New and old are locked in a struggle of 'creative destruction' (Stacey 1996: 174). I develop this idea further in the context of attractors and fractals in Chapter 6. We are here dealing with one of the essential control parameters of a non-linear dynamical system, namely the degree of *diversity of the schemas* that are driving behaviour in the system. We have seen in Chapter 3 that it is only when these control parameters reach certain values that the system can operate in the phase transition and occupy the creative learning zone.

If I had been pursuing only an orthodox professional learning programme, then I would have avoided any suggestion of this form of deep learning in the recessive schema of the college. This might have led to a quieter life. How far we did reach into this shadow learning system is hard to gauge.

In brief, therefore, I hoped to create in our PD work not just another formal legitimate and deterministic system to deliver predictable outcomes, but to explore ways of creating an adaptive feedback network capable of deep learning, which in turn would lead to a change in the college's culture and modify the control parameters that affect the state of the system.

It is sometimes easier first to describe situations when such deep learning did *not* and could not occur, in other words when we were avoiding deep learning. Deep and complex learning is frequently avoided by the very formal strategies that management so often adopts and that are such a popular item of school effectiveness and improvement. Indeed, legitimate systems exist to maintain and defend the status quo. Frequently these strategies make the implicit assumption that the route to change must be from one equilibrium state to another, more desirable, equilibrium state by means of a change from one set of normative structures and procedures to another. For example, I had found that the mere introduction of a factorial approach to improvement could lead to changes on the surface. However, once one had introduced changes such as a tutorial system, a referral system, professional development and so on there was a tendency for the system to formalize and, therefore, neutralize the ongoing potential of innovation so that it became 'more of the same'. Once the new tutorial system had been up and running for several months I recorded in my diary that many tutorial classes were operating just like ordinary 'lectures'. This was the learned behaviour that the teacher understood. In a number of groups there was little interaction or meaningful engagement around issues of personal progress or pastoral matters. New behaviours concerning pastoral care were not yet learned or were feared and, therefore, defended against; the same was true of PD sessions. When staff members were asked to plan and lead these sessions there was a strong tendency to revert to the formal lecture, as we have seen above.

Novelty is *anxiety*-provoking because it leads individuals and groups into states of disequilibrium and therefore defensive behaviours kick in to protect against the new and restore a stable, equilibrium state. There is a powerful tendency in human organizations to avoid the space for creativity because it leads to *anxiety*; our experience leads us to dislike complex learning, and we are much more comfortable with normal, legitimate learning styles. We frequently seek ways of destroying our own deep learning through what are often semi-conscious avoidance strategies involving fantasy and defensive mechanisms (Stacey 1996). When this is allowed to happen, as I have illustrated above, then no matter how intensive, well researched or impressive the improvement or effectiveness programme is, the system will relentlessly keep reproducing the same behaviours and patterns; it will reproduce itself because there is no alteration, replication or mutation of schemas at a deep level.

Without a doubt there are powerful forces at work to avoid complex learning and, therefore, change and anxiety. The tendency to avoid the space for creativity is strong. It is uncomfortable, and the familiar and known feels safer, more stable, and freer from *anxiety* and in balance.

In my structuring of PD days I increasingly sought ways to break up the normal symmetries and patterns of sessions. The norm was staff sitting in formal ranks in the library or staffroom receiving some formal input in the form of a talk delivered by the principal or other senior staff member. I would increasingly build in discussion time, group work and workshop-type sessions where small groups would go off to special settings to engage with certain issues. Feedback and my own observations taught me that frequently groups would stray from the formal legitimate agenda and discuss topics that were more hidden and recessive. This was fine. The formal agenda provided the main structure, but groups would explore – tentatively at first – other areas that were of concern. Some of this concern was resistance to the sorts of changes I, as principal, was trying to encourage. This was not altogether helpful to my change agenda. One senior and very traditional member of staff would frequently express reservations about the changes. Sometimes he was open and at other times covert. I recorded in my diary that he 'came up to me after a PD session and said, "Principal, your ideas are very interesting, but of course if we adopted them our examination results will get worse."' This was said in the context of a highly traditional examination system.

It is clear that the college had been operating for some considerable time primarily in the stable zone. This means that the control parameters of the system were below optimal levels. For example, *information* flows had been slow and the management culture had been remote and secretive. *Connectivity* had not been very rich. Staff had limited roles in the hierarchy, and interaction between groups and levels in the college was very limited indeed. As a result there were few opportunities to develop new networks or links. Edwardes College was a rather closed society, and there appeared to be a powerful conformity of behaviour with a strong uniformity of schemas. *Power differentials* were considerable and used in essentially authoritarian ways. *Anxiety* seemed to be low, maybe because of very defensive and rigid structures and formal and set routines of practice. This was, therefore, an institution that was avoiding deep, complex learning and the creative zone. Some staff members – a minority – were dipping into the shadow system where they were colluding to sustain the current stable, legitimate system in its highly stable state. They were using the shadow system to resist change and maintain the legitimate system. Only when the shadow system works against the legitimate system will an organization be able to change in deep and complex ways. It seems that there was not sufficient creative tension between the legitimate and shadow systems. Unless something was done about that no amount of normal management and change processes would produce the sorts of change and learning required.

Staff were able to play in the shadow or recessive system, as it were, between the cracks of the formal legitimate agenda of our PD programme. However, I did try out more adventurous new patterns of engagement. On one occasion, during a visit of five visitors from Birmingham, I deliberately set up a full staff session in the main hall with everyone, including the principal and all the 'hierarchy', sitting in a large circle. Suddenly all appeared equal. The 'hierarchy' had temporarily been 'abolished'. Professional and personal 'distances' had been equalized. The juniors found themselves sitting next to the most senior, and some found themselves sitting next to strangers from Birmingham. This very experience was itself a powerful, deep learning experience. Individuals would be interrogating their own interior schemas about a situation that was new to them and to which they were not sure how to react. The circle temporarily and symbolically altered the control parameters. *Anxiety* was heightened, *connectivity* and communications were suddenly greatly increased, *power differentials* were dramatically flattened and enriched varieties of behavioural *schemas* were drawn out.

The ostensible or primary task of this circular session was to consider the issue of quality and the possibility of setting up 'quality circles' in various specified areas of the college's work. No doubt all were expecting the usual pattern of the principal giving some formal input or talk, which would have allowed staff to adopt a passive, defensive role and either listen or not. Instead, participants were first of all asked to engage with their neighbour on an issue involving quality. Then individuals were given the opportunity to express themselves to the whole group. This was followed by small-group interaction still occupying the circular forum after which the groups made submissions to the plenary.

Irrespective of the topic, this format of learning contained its own implicit learning opportunities offering the chance to behave in new and unfamiliar ways. Perhaps most importantly, individuals found they had to engage with others with whom they would normally never communicate except in a formal structural mode.

It is interesting to note that at about this time the computer science department held a number of regular important meetings, consulting widely among the staff but crucially with the director of studies and vice-principal. They then approached me to suggest a major and important new curricular innovation which was taken forward to produce a most fruitful new set of high-quality courses. Whether the PD sessions had helped to create a new set of behavioural schemas that gave these staff members the confidence to explore new ventures with the risks and anxieties attached is hard to tell. But genuine learning and creative innovation was taking place, and that was a new departure in the predominantly defensive culture that had dominated for so long. Such spontaneous self-organization proved in this case highly creative, but was regarded with suspicion by the leading defensive hierarchs. However, it did represent a start in the process of play in the shadow system against the formal legitimate system.

Having experienced and participated in these various forms of professional interactions and forums, I found it interesting to observe senior staff plan and implement their own PD sessions. I was keen that staff should be empowered to run their own PD. As remarked, most of them reverted almost immediately to highly structured and formal lecture sessions of the traditional pattern. This effectively killed off any complex learning, and all deep learning was avoided, while at the same time everyone was able to believe that learning was taking place. Once again everyone had their proper allotted place, the hierarchy was restored and the anxiety of deep complex learning and Model II behaviour was avoided through defensive routines and behaviours.

In an important sense the college was adopting consciously and unconsciously a theory-in-use of its own purpose and identity that seemed to say: 'We are a family, and the college is here to provide us with security and life long employment. We are here to provide education in the time-honoured way, and traditional ways are the best. Everyone has his or her own place determined solely by seniority. The system exists to maintain the status quo.' Theories-in-use in the context of 'actionable knowledge' are discussed in detail by Argyris (1999: 297) (see Chapter 3), who claims as a baseline that: 'The task of any theory-in-use of managing is to produce generalizations that are actionable by managers in everyday life and that as managers use such generalizations, they create opportunities for robust tests of their validity.'

The struggle for change, real institutional learning and professional development depended on whether this deeply held and largely unconscious defensive theory-in-use could be transformed into something much more dynamic and life-giving. Indeed, the heart of the matter was whether the staff were able to play in the shadow system in such a way as to occupy the space for creativity positively, not avoid it and not at the same time trigger chaos and confusion.

6 Lessons and principles for schools from Dynamical Systems Theory

Never doubt that a small group of thoughtful, committed citizens can change the world. Indeed, it is the only thing that ever has.

Margaret Mead

The central theme of this book can be summarized briefly as follows. Traditional management frameworks and traditional approaches to school effectiveness and improvement have yielded disappointing results, partly because they are based upon an incomplete and inadequate theoretical and methodological framework. Traditional SEI approaches have taken an essentially linear, mechanistic and 'intentionalist' approach in which the primary focus is on *inputs* and *outputs* (factorial approach). This has generated a prime question: *'How can we design and run our schools to yield successful outcomes?'* The model is a mechanistic one dealing with schools as if they were like machines: press this button, get this result.

Fundamentally, I have been calling for a shift away from a prime focus on quantitative measures of educational outcomes and highly specific, frequently measured inputs in the form of factors, policies and procedures. Instead, Dynamical Systems Theory (DST) calls for a greater – or at least equal – emphasis upon the state of the system, on what I have called system parameters. This implies an acceptance of the complex, unpredictable, messy and self-organizing character of schools. Dynamical Systems Theory calls for less technical-rational approaches and more complexity, organic, relational, non-linear approaches.

Traditional management has focused upon *intended* and even *mandated* outcomes. There is nothing wrong with that in itself. But the new approach of Dynamical Systems Theory places a prime, or at least equal, focus on system states that can engender creativity, learning and the wonderful morale that can come about when people work together in richly creative environments where individuals become originators and experience a high level of personal causation. I suspect a great deal of the low morale alluded to earlier stems from uncreative working environments.

Let us therefore try to look at what this can mean in practice within schools and school systems. An important function of leadership in schools is to understand and be able to modulate the five key *control parameters*, which reflect and create the overall state of the system (or what complexity science calls the 'attractor' or 'strange attractor'):

1 Rate and quality of information and energy flow through the system
2 Richness of connectivity between agents in the system
3 Level of diversity within and between the behavioural schemas of the agents
4 Power differentials within the system and their modes of expression
5 Level of anxiety that can be held and contained in the system.

Managing and modulating these control parameters is what Morgan (1997) calls 'The art of managing "context"'. Dynamical Systems Theory shows that a crucial role of managers in education is to help create contexts and system states where self-organization and creativity can occur. Leaders will do well to understand the system parameters that dictate the 'context' or 'attractor' and state of the system and should develop skill in modulating and shaping those parameters. They will also have to learn the difficult lesson of leaving details of change to unfold within this context and framework. The essence of this is to avoid retaining too much control while at the same time actively contributing to the shaping of the emergent qualities and system states through creating the optimum context. I hope this book has contributed to our understanding of ways in which Dynamical Systems Theory can be useful in helping to understand schools and similar organizations.

The insights that have emerged from this discussion have significant implications for leadership and management. One of the most important insights concerns agency and instrumentalism. Current frames of management thinking encourage us to think in terms of making specific inputs to produce predetermined, intended and often zero-defect outputs in linear mode. Dynamical Systems Theory suggests a different emphasis. My discussion here has been based upon practice, theory and philosophy which suggest that, in the process of system 'cognition' leading to change and development, inputs and outputs, while clearly important, are, in the new paradigm, set alongside 'relations' and system 'dynamics'. Traditional methodologies have focused on inputs and outputs with less concern for relations and contexts. In short, the new approach calls for a greater emphasis on *means* and a proportionally lesser one on *ends*.

Table 4.1, in Chapter 4 on 'Micro-politics and the shadow system', brings together many of the elements we have explored so far in an attempt to provide a working map of the organizational context. It provides practitioners in schools with a guide to the emotional and organizational elements that will be crucial for a learning organization.

Table 6.1 Balance of inputs, outcomes and relations in organizations

1 Context/inputs (from environment)	2 Relations/process (self-organizing, closed elements)	3 Intended outcomes (to environment)
People	Connectivity	Fulfilled educational aims
Money	Power differentials	Examination and test results
Materials	Collegiality	Qualitative student outcomes
Information	Holding anxiety	Fulfilled life chances of students
Ideas, policy, wider culture	Variety of schemas	Rich engagement with community
Expertise	Rate of information flow	

Table 6.1 illustrates the three basic elements of an organization. What I have attempted to depict is what is referred to in autopoiesis theory as an *organizationally* 'closed' system, which is at the same time open with regard to the flow of resources, people, ideas and energy. For present purposes it may be better to describe it as a 'bounded' system. Columns 1 and 3 refer to the aspects of the system – its inputs and outcomes – whose prime orientation is towards the outside environment. Column 2 has more to do with the self-organizing and autopoietic nature of the system whose prime, though not exclusive, orientation may be said to be towards the internal, autonomous workings of the system and its self-making and sustaining processes.

We have seen that an important consequence of the application of autopoiesis to organizations is a radically new understanding of the relation of an organization and its environment. Traditional understandings of organizational theory have viewed a system and its environment as very different entities with change normally originating in the environment. According to this view, the system is 'open' to its environment and interacts with it by constantly turning inputs (Column 1) into outputs (Column 3) in order to survive and compete. This whole idea is challenged by Dynamical Systems Theory and Complexity Theory, which view the system as having a primary function of self-making and self-producing through a 'closed' system of relations even though in other respects it remains open to and engaged with its environment. If this is accepted, then it is clear that the most important – though not the only – product of the system is the system itself. This is achieved through the processes and dynamics enumerated in Column 2 of Table 6.1. Even a system's interaction with its environment is actually a part of its own self-making. Its environment is in reality a part of itself.

I have explored in some detail behaviour in the legitimate and shadow systems (Chapter 3), and this allows me to delineate and define these systems more precisely now. I start with the understanding that human systems (individuals, groups, organizations and societies) are all non-linear networks nesting within one another. Merry (1995) uses the colourful description of complex systems as 'a set of wooden Russian dolls, each containing a smaller replica of itself within'. Individual systems contain what I have described in this book as two crucial sub-systems.

The legitimate system

In the legitimate system, behaviour engages with current reality – that is, with the immediate demands or mandates or explicit aims and functions of the system – and is driven by dominant schema that are shared by all, or most, agents within the system. This leads to a high degree of conformity. I have shown some of the ways in which the legitimate system worked at Edwardes College and UTS to deliver what is defined (Bion 1961) as 'work group' behaviour, which is concerned with the overt, legitimate tasks and mandates of the system. For example, at Edwardes College and UTS our explicit legitimate tasks involved the delivery, in different settings, of high-quality educational outcomes. These legitimate tasks are either the outcome of intentions formally established by the most powerful and influential members of the organization – the principal, senior managers, governors and founders – or are established through well-understood principles widely accepted within it. The legitimate system and work-group behaviour comprise the primary task through which the organization competes and survives. Its survival depends on getting other organizations and individuals to interact with it. In the legitimate system, outputs (Column 3 in Table 6.1) are usually proportional to inputs (Column 1 in Table 6.1). Once the shadow system comes into play the inputs and outputs can be quite disproportional.

The shadow system

In the shadow system, 'recessive' schemas rather than current reality or legitimate tasks, aims and mandates drive system behaviour. Most recessive schemas belong to individuals and therefore have a tendency to lead to diversity. In the shadow system, individuals interact spontaneously and informally around issues not usually connected with official agendas, and often the system contains a more political flavour. In the shadow, agents develop their own private rules for interacting with each other. This leads to the formation of a non-legitimate culture not sanctioned by the official legitimate system. UTS provided a good example of this sort of counter-legitimate culture where shadow system activity and recessive schemas had achieved a dominance over the formal, official and legitimate structure and system. In this context the 'primary' task was to a considerable extent diverted and the micro-political climate shifted towards the turbulent and chaotic. I have described some of this sort of activity in relation to professional development activity in Chapter 5 and micro-political activity in Chapter 4. The resistance Group X at Edwardes College operated in this way and were influenced by internal and external cultural rules that were not officially sanctioned. This may have been exacerbated to some degree by the fact that I was an expatriate not fully subject or sensitive to these shadow rules drawn from the local cultures.

By definition these alternative or recessive rules or schemas do not derive from the current primary task. It would be wrong to characterize these recessive or shadow rules as necessarily negative forces. The shadow system is in effect a body of thoughts, behaviours, ideas and perceptions which are potential and available but not currently in use in the legitimate system. The shadow system is difficult to understand and pin down. Its purposes, in the words of Stacey (1996), 'range from petty politicking to unofficial efforts to support or sabotage the legitimate system'. My description of the most creative phase of our development programme at Edwardes College shows positive learning and an atmosphere of creativity. At this stage I sensed that parts of the shadow system associated with Group Z were working to promote the explicit aims of the legitimate system. However, at the same time other elements associated with resistance Group X were using the shadow system to frustrate the aims of the legitimate system and Group Z. Leadership involves representing the legitimate system while at the same time being aware of shadow-system activity and cultivating creative activity in the shadow system. Much more work will have to be done on this to make it a fully operative part of good leadership practice.

Theoretical understandings

As a result of our explorations of Dynamical Systems Theory (DST) we are led to a new prime question facing educators, which can be expressed as follows: *How far does the experience of managing change help illustrate principles of design, leadership and practice in school contexts of complexity, and how can new understandings of complex dynamical systems assist in activating and realizing the space for creativity (phase transition) – the so-called 'edge of chaos' where deep system learning is possible?* This of course begs many other questions. My theoretical conclusions have drawn upon, and attempt to bring together, the different theoretical traditions we have explored throughout. These are insights from complexity and chaos theory, the theory of autopoiesis and organizational psychodynamics. In applying this theory (much of which has been developed in the physical sciences) to human organizations, I have adopted many of the concepts in the context of a metaphorical understanding to help illuminate the reality of organizational behaviour in schools. These metaphors can provide powerful new ways of thinking about schools as organizations. Outlined below are five of the essential understandings to emerge from the new prime question I have posed.

1 Cause and effect

Schools change over time. Some changes are planned and proceed smoothly, while others occur abruptly without warning. We have learned that exact prediction within organizations is difficult if not impossible.

Cause and effect are, therefore, not always closely related. Actions taken with the intention of effecting specific changes sometimes fail to create such an effect within the expected time frame or may never achieve identifiable results. Our attempts in Edwardes College PD sessions to affect classroom practice yielded only patchy results. Some staff responded with enthusiasm; others not at all. Major interventions may produce insignificant results and small interventions significant ones. Our interventions in classroom practice gave relatively minor results; our interventions on pastoral care greater results; the board of governors' intervention in the school towards the end of the programme vast and unexpected results. A similar postulate suggests that changes in one part of a system affect other system components in unexpected ways. For example, the creation of a much strengthened SMT with enhanced allowances for post holders had a positive effect on a wide range of activities, but at the same time it caused resentment to build up among certain senior staff members who did not like seeing less senior staff having responsibility, and this led to resistance to change. In 'edge of chaos' 'far from equilibrium' situations, small but critical actions at the appropriate time can result in major and transforming effects, while the same action in a more stable equilibrium state may have virtually nil effect. This suggests that timing and concentration upon system states are important.

2 Fractal nature

Institutions can be said to have a fractal nature. Fractal refers to qualities that are 'self-similar'. In the case of organizations this means that systems are holographic or fractal such that the parts interact continually to recreate the whole and the operation of the whole affects the interaction and functioning of the parts. 'Fractal' means that behaviours, patterns, structures and processes will be similar at small group, department, divisional, and whole institutional levels. It is this repetition (and high level of redundancy) of patterned process that is able to give fit and context for mission and vision. Where there is little fractal self-similarity it is harder to create shared aims and goals.

A further important aspect of fractal nature is the very process of 'iteration' or repetition. Fractal geometry deals with the 'folding' and repeating of functions. In a metaphorical sense this is illuminating for organizations because the endless repetition of interactions is in itself a creative process. Through a process of repeating, knowledge and understanding become 'enfolded' and, therefore, 'implicit' as opposed to 'unfolded' or 'explicit'. Such a process embeds behaviours, understandings and knowledge in an organization. A theory of flux and change and of *implicate* order and *explicate* order has been developed by the theoretical physicist David Bohm (1980, 1987). With reference to the management of schools, Fullan (1999) and Nonaka and Tacheuchi (1995) develop the similar concept of *tacit* and *explicit* knowledge.

3 Feedback and system states

Institutions are 'attracted' to identifiable states through a process of 'positive' and 'negative' feedback which creates a dynamic equilibrium. I have attempted to show that, when a system is in stable equilibrium, its behaviour is comparatively simple. As complexity increases due to increasing levels of system control parameters, periodicity or cycling behaviour arises; and as states of the control parameters rise even further, behaviour can become random or chaotic. I have identified five control parameters that are crucial to schools: *information flow, connectivity, diversity, power differentials and anxiety*. Many of the changes we introduced at Edwardes College led to increases in these control parameters (one might describe it as the tempo or intensity at which we were 'running' the institution) and this in turn led to changes in the overall state of the institution from rigidity towards creativity and eventually towards chaos and high turbulence. At UTS, in a sense a sort of reverse process was set in motion with the attempt to dampen down the high levels of political 'noise' and the chaotic characteristics that had emerged. I have shown above how changes to the control parameters affect the system state. For example, new assessment and reporting procedures represent increases in *information flow*; new management structures can lead to changes in *variety, anxiety* and *power differentials*. Perhaps one of the most important features of complex systems is feedback. The learning loop of *discovery, choice* and *action* is the central feedback process. Feedback, as we have seen, can be either 'negative' or 'positive'. It is essential to understand that these terms are not used here in the colloquial sense of 'good' and 'bad' in the sense that one might say, 'I have had some negative feedback on the performance of the third-year students this term' – meaning bad information. 'Negative' here is understood in the technical sense of homeostatic or self-regulating – that is, tending to a norm. 'Positive' is understood to mean amplifying. It should be emphasized that the terms 'positive' and 'negative' have no value connotation whatsoever. In order to avoid misunderstanding, I will therefore use the terms 'self-regulating' and 'self-amplifying' in preference to the potentially ambiguous complex systems terms 'negative' and 'positive'.

4 Self-regulating (negative) feedback

This occurs when a system has some prior or external or systemic intention, plan or requirement. As the system implements the plan it uses the discovery, choice and action cyclical feedback loop to check outcomes against the targets. Information regarding progress is fed back into the system to rectify any deviations. This is what is usually referred to as monitoring. Self-regulating feedback is, therefore, the control of intentional development or required states. It damps down deviations in the pursuit of a planned change or course of action and seeks stability and predictability, and is the prime form of feedback in 'legitimate' systems pursuing a primary task. This kind of feedback is essentially homeostatic. A human body employs negative feedback to maintain a constant normal body temperature.

5 Self-amplifying (positive) feedback

This occurs when a system uses the cycles of discovery, choice and action in a manner that amplifies changes and destabilizes that system. In the human organization this often operates in political modes and through grapevines as well as highly creative (or destructive) cultures. The 'shadow' system is often driven by self-amplifying (positive) feedback, but it can also be dominated by self-regulating (negative) feedback, as for example when some college staff used the shadow system to maintain old ways of doing things that the legitimate system was trying to change.

In order to clarify the distinction between the two types of feedback, the following simple definitions are helpful. Self-amplifying feedback occurs when a causal influence from 'A' to 'B' leads to a change in 'A' producing a change in 'B' in the same direction. In other words, 'B' increases if 'A' increases and 'B' decreases if 'A' decreases. The feedback is self-regulating if 'B' changes in the opposite direction. In other words 'B' decreases when 'A' increases and 'B' increases when 'A' decreases. Self-amplifying feedback can be said to be 'deviation-amplifying' – in other words, its effects lead away from the norm – and self-regulating feedback is 'self-correcting' or 'self-dampening', tending always towards a norm. It is surprising that feedback – especially self-amplifying feedback – has only recently been explored in detail because it has been implicit in much work in the social sciences throughout their history. Perhaps the most famous example of self-regulation is Adam Smith's 'invisible hand' regulating the market economy. By contrast, popular terms such as 'vicious and virtuous circles', 'self-fulfilling prophecies', 'the bandwagon effect' and 'runaway inflation' all express the phenomenon of self-amplifying feedback.

At Edwardes College, academic assessment and record-keeping had the dual role of both self-amplifying and self-regulating feedback. It was self-amplifying in the sense that it created a sort of bandwagon effect leading to greater seriousness in study by students and in teaching by staff (a sort of competitiveness). It was self-regulating in that it allowed those who were failing to be identified and brought back on track for academic success (self-correcting). Real institutional effectiveness and creativity require a balance of self-regulatory and self-amplifying feedback. Planned changes will require careful monitoring (self-regulation). If the change or initiative goes off course, feedback must be used to help bring it back to the 'norm'. This happened in many instances at Edwardes College, for example in the implementation of new student records, a new pastoral system, and new methods and procedures for assessment. If something was not working as planned, we fed the information back through decision-making bodies to rectify things. If the feedback suggested the original plan was faulty, amendments were made to the operation.

There were examples of self-regulating feedback that were also 'negative' in a value sense; for example, our efforts to introduce new, more student-centred and interactive styles of classroom teaching were limited by a self-regulatory process. The style of exams, the unwillingness of many to change the habits of a lifetime, the resisters of change and the large class sizes combined to create feedback that prevented much change of practice in the classroom. What we needed in this instance was a self-amplifying process that could enable teachers to break away from a very powerful norm of traditional teaching styles. We needed a bandwagon effect or a virtuous circle where the example of a few, who were moving onto new and more creative methods, would induce and inspire more and more staff to follow suit. Once teachers have begun to use new methods, self-regulatory feedback, possibly in the form of professional development activity and peer counselling, will help keep the changes on track.

6 Phase transition or creative state

There is a state known as a phase transition which I have identified as the 'creative state' where real creativity becomes possible. A number of expressions are used in the literature for this enigmatic entity, including 'space for creativity', 'creative zone', 'edge of chaos' and 'far-from-equilibrium'. Though not ideal, I have preferred the expression 'creative state'. I have hypothesized that this creative state occurs when the state of the control parameters reach optimal levels and a sublime balance is achieved between stability and instability and between self-amplifying and self-regulating feedback. This has important implications for leadership and policymaking. The data assembled in this study strongly suggest that with increasing tempo the system experiences more turbulence and more creativity. The data also show that instances of staff interacting in creative ways greatly increased as we progressed with our changes. A greater variety of professional behaviour and practice was observed as new methods were tried. More and better-quality information became available. There was a higher level of connectivity and interaction. Power and influence became more widely dispersed, and through all this anxiety levels increased and needed containment and caring for. The data also suggest that if levels of these control parameters become too high, mild turbulence can tip over into conditions of randomness and chaos.

Some organizational theorists have used the term 'attractor' and 'strange attractor' to describe and explain the extraordinary dynamic configuration that takes place in this state (Waldrop 1992, Morgan 1997, Stacey 1996). Complexity theorists have suggested that complex systems can fall under the influence or pull of different types of 'attractor'. Human organizations can also fall under the influence of 'attractors'. I prefer to use the term 'attractor' in a metaphorical sense when discussing human organizations. At its simplest level, one might say that Edwardes College was under the sway of a simple 'attractor' pulling it constantly towards the norms of traditional teaching and stable organizational norms. As we moved forward with our change programme we approached a phase transition where a new 'attractor' began to pull the system towards new configurations, learnings, dynamics and destinations centred on new styles of teaching and new institutional structures and processes.

These attractors tend to define the context in which the detailed behaviours of the system unfold. Used metaphorically in human systems, they offer a useful aid to an understanding of system behaviour. At the start of the change programme at Edwardes College I suggested that the institution was in the stuck and/or promenading state or a sort of point/ periodic attractor. Routines and behaviour were largely predictable within the limits of a certain context or 'attractor'. This included matters such as teaching styles, timetables, examinations, and management processes. By the time we had reached the most creative phase of the change process, new 'attractors' could be felt in the form of new behaviours, new aspirations and expectations, new models and new visions for the future. These can be described metaphorically as basins of attraction. The first was constantly pulling us back into tried and tested old ways. The second was beckoning to new worlds of professional practice and a new self-image for the institution. True to dynamical systems theory, the system entered a turbulent phase transition where it flipped or 'bifurcated' or oscillated between the old and the new 'attractors'. Sometimes the progressives were winning; sometimes the traditionalists.

7 Self-organization and emergence

The concept of self-organization (in a school context, 'self-ordering' might be better) and emergence go together and are of great importance in dynamical systems theory. Students, teachers and management interact to give rise to a particular institutional behaviour, which contributes to the nature, environment and culture of the system. This interaction among members of the community gives rise to the emergence of surprising and often unpredictable behaviours such as, for example, academic rigour, caring or charitable giving. This manifestation of 'emergence' arises from 'self-organization', which is the spontaneous generation of order (and sometimes disorder) from within an open system. This is what Kauffman (1993) calls, 'order for free'. This sort of order, therefore, arises most naturally from within the system, not through imposition from outside. As agents interact they organize themselves according to local parameters and self-interest out of which a higher, more global structure emerges. It is perhaps the local parameters that are crucial in management terms.

If we take a school as an example, academic rigour can come from students meeting together in study groups, teachers preparing interesting and challenging work and projects, and management purchasing important equipment. Alternatively, it can come from sound reporting procedures, and assessment methods and parental involvement. Whatever the magic ingredients for improvement, they cannot be fully organized from outside the school without some element of self-organizing creativity from within. Fullan (1993) expresses this differently by saying: 'You can't mandate what matters (the more complex the change the less you can force it).' In any system there may be a mixture of self-organization and intervention or imposition. This relates to the crucial matter of how a system and its environment interact or co-evolve. Examination syllabuses, budgets and curricula are often externally imposed, while methods of delivery, teaching styles, aspects of the curriculum (including the hidden curriculum and relationships) can be – though often are not – the outcome of self-organization.

We saw examples of self-organization at Edwardes College when, for example, the computer science department devised a scheme to introduce new courses, new tests and new methods of professional operation within the department. Other examples included the spontaneous reordering of the management of examinations by a small group within the SMT or the spontaneous tightening of record-keeping by the year heads or the pressure for a small staff development group among younger staff after one of the regular professional development visits to Birmingham. There are many other examples. Self-amplifying feedback caused these initiatives to be devised, and self-regulating feedback helped them to remain on track once they were up and running.

What dynamical systems theory suggests – and what my data and experience seem to confirm – is that the balance between self-organization and external imposition is important. We may hypothesize that too much imposition or intervention can have the effect of stifling creativity and natural self-organizing tendencies. Too much self-organization, if not coherent, may lead to elements of randomness and chaos as a lack of direction begins to be felt. It is here that the 'fractal' nature of the system comes into play. If there is a high degree of fractal 'self-similarity' (see above) across the institution allowing staff in all sections and departments to share behaviours, discourses, values, operating structures and procedures, then high degrees of self-organization may be more sustainable without the risk of anarchy. In the case of Edwardes College it was difficult to create this fractal self-similarity, at least to begin with. Some staff members had a positive outlook and were willing to learn and change; some were not. A small element – what I have called the group of resisters – sought ways to oppose the change programme. In order to achieve a culture of learning and creativity and responsibility it was necessary to create these echoing, repeating discourses and a dynamic in which the whole affects and informs the parts and vice versa. At the most positive and creative stages of the programme high levels of fractal self-similarity and creativity were achieved.

Lessons for leaders in schools

The ideas explored in this book lead to a number of practical conclusions for practitioners. These will need further research and testing on the ground.

1 **Traditional strategic planning, action planning and grand designs are problematical** and may be counterproductive due to the inherently unpredictable nature of human organizations. A sense of direction is important, but a rigid blueprint of the future is often counterproductive. School managers must develop a radically new mindset that has the confidence to allow for uncertainty and the space for creativity and that is not too eager to control details of change. We have seen how order can evolve as an emergent property as new 'attractors' develop. The new emphasis may seem frightening and unwelcome to school leaders used to the orthodoxies of planning, structures, hierarchies and input–output models that allow more of a sense of control.

2 **Vision and mission cannot be mandated or imposed.** They must grow and be nurtured. Vision and mission will not flourish unless the system moves towards the 'creative state', and this can be achieved through concentrating in the first place upon the state of the system control parameters. Vision and mission have a much better chance of taking root and developing if the organization has a positively 'fractal' structure and pattern so that values, thinking, practice and behaviour are self-similar and repeated and echoed throughout the system in reinforcing loops and interactions. Such 'fractals' might be histories and traditions, but also can revolve around acceptance of basic human rights, values and responsibilities. There will be some matters of values and rights, such as equity and inclusivity, which are not negotiable.

3 **The learning or intelligent school is one that has effective and balanced self-amplifying (positive) and self-regulating (negative) feedback loops.** The cyclical process of feedback is central to system 'cognition'. Management will need to understand in detail the effects and processes

of different forms of feedback in order to encourage deep and lasting institutional learning.

4   **One of the most important features of a learning organization is the quality and quantity of interactions between members of the community.** This may seem obvious but, with the much more detailed knowledge now available about how complex dynamical systems work, practitioners can create environments where creative interaction is maximized. Research has shown that in a creative organization human interactions have an extraordinary power both for creativity and destructiveness. In both cases one plus one can equal much more than two. An understanding of how to foster powerfully creative interactions is vital to modern management in new complexity paradigms.

5   **Leadership has a dual responsibility regarding the levels of anxiety in the system.** Anxiety is inescapable and even necessary in an environment of innovation and change. On one hand the leadership, indeed all members of the community, must create a culture and atmosphere in which all the members feel cared for, valued and encouraged and where creativity and its attendant risks are also encouraged. This is a culture where *mistakes and failures* are tolerated, even expected, but where *negligence* is not. In such an environment members are more likely to take anxiety-inducing innovative and creative steps. The untried and the new always bring with them uncertainty and anxiety, and there is no change without some anxiety. By the same token we have seen that anxiety is the paramount variable control parameter. In certain system states, practitioners may need to provoke anxieties actively. This might normally occur at the early stages of a change programme in a system that is in a very rigid and stable state where system control parameters are at low levels. Anxiety may also arise in groups where group development is at an early stage and individual group members are unsure of themselves and their colleagues. These were exactly the sorts of situation that existed at Edwardes College when I started. Naturally, at the same time as provoking anxiety it will be necessary to take steps to mitigate that anxiety by creating a caring and 'holding' environment so that this anxiety does not convert itself into shadow-system activity aimed at opposing the anxiety-inducing changes.

Sometimes anxiety will take the form of a sense of threat. An individual might see a change as a threat to his or her position. This sort of anxiety can lead to potent micro-political activity and use of the shadow system. Just as leaders may need to provoke anxiety at certain times, so also at others they may need to damp down anxiety positively by slowing or even stopping changes. Change should stop or be radically slowed down when it provokes so much anxiety that the system becomes dysfunctional and unstable; in such a dysfunctional state the system control parameters will have reached high levels and should be reduced urgently.

6 **Double-loop learning and real creativity are unlikely to occur unless the system parameters are managed and modulated into optimum states.** Practitioners will need to focus on aspects of their schools and devise measures to guide the institution into the 'creative space'. We have seen that these parameters are:

a) *information flow*. Rate of flow and quality of information and its availability;
b) *variety and diversity*. A rich variety of practice and behaviour without too much latitude, which could lead to anarchic and random conditions;
c) *power differentials*. Where responsibility is delegated to provide a wide range of centres of influence without becoming so devolved and democratic that nobody is in charge and the system becomes immobilized through lack of effective decision-making processes;
d) *connectivity* or the processes of engagement and involvement between individuals and groups. This engagement is often in the form of affective ties such as loyalty, affection and collegiality.

These four parameters can be systematically and consciously modulated. They all interact with each other and their state has a direct effect upon the fifth crucial variable – *anxiety*. This is what Morgan (1997) calls 'the art of managing and changing "context"'. A crucial role of managers in education is to help create contexts and system states in which self-organization and creativity can occur. I have shown that managers will do well to understand the system parameters that dictate the 'context' and 'attractor' and state of the system and should develop skill in modulating and shaping those parameters. Managers will also have to learn to sometimes leave details to unfold within this context and frame. The essence of this is avoiding too much control while at the same time actively contributing to the shaping of the emergent qualities and system states through creating the optimum context.

Morgan (1997: 267) describes the management of context as follows:

> Managers have to become skilled in helping to shape parameters that can define an appropriate context, while allowing the details to unfold within this frame. In this way, they can help to shape emergent processes of self-organization, while avoiding the trap of too much control ... *transformational change ultimately involves the creation of 'new contexts' that can break the hold of dominant attractor patterns in favour of new ones.*
>
> (Author's italics)

The new management will not be able to control all the details of change. That is not a possibility. New attractors will take their own form. Managers can nurture and shape the system parameters: information flow, connectivity, diversity, power differentials and anxiety levels. The manager helps to create the conditions and context for new states or attractors to emerge.

7   **Of very great significance for the school effectiveness and improvement movement and for public policy is the matter of the relations and interactions between individual schools and the wider educational environment.** This is a large issue, especially in the UK where there has been a strong sense of excessive and suffocating intervention in schools from government. Policymakers and practitioners can do much to assist in the effective interaction between local and wider environments by understanding the nature of autopoietic and allopoietic systems. This means that policymakers and researchers in the wider environment will need to understand and make allowance for the internal self-organizing nature of individual schools and colleges. This may call for a realization that a complex dynamical system and its environment are effectively one system (organizationally bounded but open to its environment) and that certain strategies will be needed to allow for external pressure and support while other strategies are required to cultivate and support the self-organizing creativity of individual schools without which the external inputs might not flourish. This may involve a deep and difficult change of mindset by policymakers and practitioners in which intentionalism, agency and a primary focus on ends (pressure and support, linear input–output models) give way to more non-linear approaches with a primary focus on means and relations and dynamic and creative process. A lot of work remains to be done on this and it will require not only technical–rational solutions but new frames of mind and approach.

8   **Great leverage can be achieved with an understanding of the principle that in the creative state minor changes can lead to major and transforming effects.** This practical insight is based upon the principle of 'Sensitive Dependence on Initial Conditions' (SDIC). Using this idea, managers can seek out practical high-leverage initiatives capable of bringing about major transformation. This will involve finding key bifurcation points of phase transitions that lie between 'attractors'. In this way it may be possible to steer the system from one attractor to a more suitable or effective 'attractor'. Organizational theorists speak increasingly of navigating or leading systems into far-from-equilibrium states in order to find these high-leverage points where the system can 'flip' or 'bifurcate' into new directions and 'attractors'. Perhaps the most important point here is that these high-leverage, highly creative states take time to create. Initiative A carried out in a stable 'attractor' state may yield negligible results. The same initiative A carried out in a far-from-equilibrium state may yield significant, creative and astonishing results. An understanding of this principle of SDIC helps managers

to cut through the intimidating complexity of modern educational management and focus on a few simple principles and ideas.

All the points outlined above relate to and contribute to the engendering of the 'creative state'. We have seen that this is an archetype which has a potentially patterned and complex behaviour with stability of shape and boundary. However, the specific actualization of the archetype is radically unpredictable.

Successful innovators in schools may benefit from an understanding of the nature of the 'creative state' archetype in organizations. I have tried to outline some of the practical steps that are needed to actualize this creative state of endless and deep innovation and creativity, which has its own inbuilt drivers as well as its constraints.

Bibliography

Alderfer, C.P. (1972) *Existence, Relatedness, and Growth: Human Needs in Organizational Settings*. New York: Free Press.

Argyris, C. (1990) *Overcoming Organizational Defences – Facilitating Organizational Learning*. Boston: Allyn and Bacon.

Argyris, C. (1999, second edn) *On Organizational Learning*. London: Blackwell.

Argyris, C. and Schon, D. (1978) *Organisational Learning: A Theory of Action Perspective*. Reading, MA: Addison-Wesley.

Arthur, W.B. (1989) 'The Economy and Complexity' in Stein, D.L. *Lectures in the Sciences of Complexity*. Redwood City, California: Addison-Wesley.

Avalos, B. (1980) 'Teacher Effectiveness: Research in the Third World: Highlights of a Review', *Comparative Education* 16: 45–54.

Avalos, B. (1985) 'Training for Better Teaching in the Third World: Lessons from Research', *Teaching and Teacher Education* 1: 289–299.

Axelrod, R. (1984) *The Evolution of Cooperation*. New York: Basic Books.

Bachrach, P. and Baratz, M.S. (1962) 'Two Faces of Power', *American Political Science Review* 54(4): 947–952.

Baddeley, A. (1990) *Human Memory: Theory and Practice*. Hove, Sussex, UK: Lawrence Erlbaum.

Bak, P. and Khan Chen (1991) 'Self-Organized Criticality', *Scientific American* January 1991: 46–53.

Baker, G.L. and Gollub, J.P. (1990) *Chaotic Dynamics: An Introduction*. Cambridge: Cambridge University Press.

Ball, S.J. (1987) *The Micro-Politics of the School: Towards a Theory of School Organisation*. London: Routledge.

Baumol, W.J. and Benhabib, J. (1989) 'Chaos: Significance, Mechanism and Economic Applications', *Journal of Economic Perspectives* 3(1): 77–105.

Beer, M., Eisenstat, R. and Spector, B. (1990) *The Critical Path to Corporate Renewal*. Boston, Mass.: Harvard Business School Press.

Berne, E. (1964) *Games People Play*. New York: Grove Press.

Bion, W.R. (1961) *Experiences in Groups, and Other Papers*. New York: Basic Books.

Bion, W.R. (1991) *Experiences in Groups and Other Papers*. London: Tavistock.

Blanchard, K. (1994) *The One-Minute Manager Builds High-Performing Teams*. London: HarperCollins.

Blanchard, K. (2001) *High Five! The Magic of Working Together*. New York: Morrow.

Blase, J. (1991) *The Politics of Life in Schools: Power, Conflict and Cooperation*. London: Sage.

Blase, J. and Anderson, G. (1995) *The Micro-politics of Educational Leadership*. London: Cassell.

Blase, J. and Blase, J. (1997) *The Fire is Back: Principals Sharing School Governance*. Thousand Oaks, CA: Corwen Press.

Bohm, D. (1980) *Wholeness and the Implicate Order*. London: Routledge & Kegan Paul.

Bohm, D. and Peat, F.D. (1987) *Science, Order and Creativity*. New York: Bantam.

Borg, W.R. (1981) *Applying Educational Research: A Practical Guide for Teachers*. New York: Longman.

Briggs, J. and Peat, F. (1989) *The Turbulent Mirror*. New York: HarperCollins.

Brodnick, R.J. and Krafft, L.J. (1997) *Chaos and Complexity Theory: Implications for Research and Planning in Higher Education*. <http://www.ship.edu/~rjbrod/complex1.html> (accessed 22 June 2000).

Brooke-Smith, R. (1999) 'Complexity and Information Feedback Systems in Schools and Colleges: Some Lessons from Pakistan'. Paper presented at International Congress for School Effectiveness and Improvement (ICSEI) Conference, San Antonio, Texas, January 1999.

Brookover, W.B. and Lezotte, L.W. (1979) *Changes in School Characteristics Coincident with Changes in Student Achievement*. East Lansing: Institute for Research on Teaching, College of Education, Michigan State University.

Brookover, W.B., Beamer, L., Afthin, H., Hathaway, D., Lezotte, L., Miller, S., Passalacqua, J. and Tornatzky, L. (1984) *Creating Effective Schools: An In-service Programme for Enhancing School Learning Climate and Environment*. Florida: Learning Publications.

Carnoy, M. (1974) *Education as Cultural Imperialism*. New York: D. McKay.

Cheng, Y.C. (1995) 'School Effectiveness and Improvement in Hong Kong, Taiwan, and Mainland China', in B.H.M. Creemers and N. Osinga, *International Congress for School Effectiveness and Improvement (ICSEI) Country Reports, Netherlands*: 11–30.

Cheng, Y.C. (1996) *School Effectiveness and School-Based Management*. London: Falmer.

Clifford, J. (1988) *The Predicament of Culture*. Cambridge, Mass.: Harvard University Press.

Cohen, L. and Manion, L. (1994) *Research Methods in Education*. London, Routledge.

Cohen, M.D., March, J.G., and Olsen, J.P. 'A Garbage Can Model of Organisational Choice', *Administrative Science Quarterly* 1972 (17): 1–25.

Coleman, J., Campbell, E., Hobson, C., McPartland, J., Mood, A., Weinfeld, F. and York, R. (1966) *Equality of Educational Opportunity*. Washington, DC: National Center for Educational Statistics/ US Government Printing Office.

Colman, A.D. and Bexton, W.H. (1975) *Group Relations Reader I*. Washington, DC: A.K. Rice Institute.

Colman, A.D. and Giller, M.H. (1985) *Group Relations Reader II*. Washington, DC: A.K. Rice Institute.

Corey, B.M. (1953) *Action Research to Improve School Practices*. New York: Columbia University Press.

Cronbach, L.J. (1988) 'Playing with Chaos', *Educational Researcher* 17(6): 46–49.

Crossley, M. and Vulliamy, G. (1997) *Qualitative Educational Research in Developing Countries*. New York: Garland.

Dahl, R.A. (1973) *Regimes and Opposition*. New Haven: Yale University Press.

Davidoff, S. and Van den Berg, O. (1990) *Changing your Teaching: The Challenge of the Classroom*. Pietermaritzburg: Centaur Publications.

Davies, L. (1990) *Equity and Efficiency: School Management in an International Context*. London: Falmer.

Davies, L. (1992) 'School Power Cultures under Economic Constraint', *Educational Review* 44: 127–136.

Davies, L. (1994) *Beyond Authoritarian School Management*. London: Education Now Books.

Davies, L. (1997a) 'The Rise of the School Effectiveness Movement', in White, J. and Barber, M. (eds) *Perspectives on School Effectiveness and School Improvement*. London: Institute of Education.

Davies, L. (1997b) 'Interviews and the Study of School Management: An International Perspective', in Crossley, M. and Vulliamy, G. (1997) op. cit.

Davies, L. (2000) 'Chaos and Complexity in the Study of School Management' in Alexander, R. and Broadfoot, P. (eds) *Learning from Comparing: New Directions in Comparative Research* 2. Oxford: Symposium Books.

Davies, P.C.W. (1987) *The Cosmic Blueprint*. London: Heinemann.

Davies, P.C.W. (ed.) (1989) *The New Physics*. New York: Cambridge University Press.

Davies, P.C.W. (1999) *The Fifth Miracle: The Search for the Origin and the Meaning of Life*. New York: Simon & Schuster.

Delamont, S. (1981) 'All Too Familiar? A Decade of Classroom Research', *Educational Analysis* 3(1): 69–83.

Deming, W.E. (1986) *Out of the Crisis*. Cambridge, MA: Massachusetts Institute of Technology.

Drakeford, B. and Cooling, J. (1998) *The Secondary Whole School Audit: Development Planning for Secondary Schools*. London: David Fulton.

Drazin, R. and Sandelands, L. (1993) 'Autogenesis: A Perspective on the Process of Organizing', *Organization Science* 3, no. 2: 230–249.

Drucker, P.F. (1993) *Post-Capitalist Society*. Oxford: Heinemann.

Edmonds, R. (1979) 'Effective School for the Urban Poor', *Educational Leadership*, October 15–34.

Elliott, J. (1991) *Action Research for Educational Change*. Buckingham: Open University Press.

Elliott, J. (1996) 'School Effectiveness Research and Its Critics: Alternative Visions of Schooling', *Cambridge Journal of Education* 26(2): 199–223.

Erikson, E. (1977) *Childhood and Society*. London: Triad/Granada.

Fitz-Gibbon, C. (1996) 'Monitoring School Effectiveness: Simplicity and Complexity' in Gray, J. *et al. Merging Traditions: The Future of Research on School Effectiveness and School Improvement*. London: Cassell.

Fitz-Gibbon, C. (1991) 'Multilevel modelling in an indicator system' in Raudenbush, S.W. *et al.* (eds) *Schools, Classrooms and Pupils: International Studies of Schooling from a Multilevel Perspective*. San Diego: Academic Press.

Foucault, M. (1977) *Power/Knowledge*. New York: Pantheon Books.

Fullan, M. (1991) *The New Meaning of Educational Change*. London: Cassell.

Fullan, M. (1992) *Successful School Improvement*. Buckingham: Open University.

Fullan, M. (1993) *Change Forces: Probing the Depths of Educational Reform*. London: Falmer Press.

Fullan, M. (1999) *Change Forces: The Sequel*. London: Falmer.

Fullan, M. (2001) *Leading in a Culture of Change*. San Francisco: Jossey-Bass.

Fullan, M. (forthcoming) *Change Forces with a Vengeance*. London: Routledge-Falmer.

Fullan, M. and Hargreaves, A. (eds) (1992) *Teacher Development and Educational Change*. London: Falmer.

Geertz, C. (1973) *The Interpretation of Cultures*. New York: Basic Books.

Gell-Mann, M. (1994) *The Quark and the Jaguar*. New York: W.H. Freeman.

Gemmell, G. and Smith, C. (1985) 'A Dissipative Structure Model of Organisational Transformation', *Human Relations* 36(8): 50–74.

Gibbard, G.S., Hartmann, J.J. and Mann, R.D. (eds) (1974) *Analysis of Groups: Contributions to Theory, Research and Practice*. San Francisco: Jossey-Bass.

Glaser, B. and Strauss, A. (1967) *The Discovery of Grounded Theory*. Chicago: Aldine.

Gleick, J. (1988) *Chaos: The Making of a New Science*. London: Heinemann.

Goldstein, H. and Myers, K. (1997) 'School Effectiveness Research: A Bandwagon, A Hijack or a Journey Towards Enlightenment?' Paper presented at British Educational Research Association meeting, York, September 1997.

Goldstein, J. (1994) *The Unshackled Organisation: Facing the Challenge of Unpredictability Through Spontaneous Reorganization*. Portland, OR, Productivity Press.

Goleman, D. (1995) *Emotional Intelligence*. New York: Bantam Books.

Goleman, D., Boyartzis, R. and McKee, A. (2002) *The New Leaders: Transforming the Art of Leadership into the Science of Results*. London: Little, Brown.

Gray, J. *et al.* (1996) *Merging Traditions: The Future of Research on School Effectiveness and School Improvement*. London: Cassell.

Gray, J., McPherson, A. and Raffe, D. (1983) *Reconstructions of Secondary Education*. London: Routledge & Kegan Paul.

Gunter, H. (1997) *Rethinking Education: The Consequences of Jurassic Management*. London: Cassell.

Gunter, H. (2001) *Leaders and Leadership in Education*. London: Paul Chapman.

Hamilton, D. (1996) 'Fordism by Fiat', *Forum* 38(2): 54–56.

Hammer, M. and Champy, J. (1993) *Reengineering the Corporation: A Manifesto for Business Revolution*. London: Bealey.

Hammersley, M. and Atkinson, P. (1983) *Ethnography: Principles and Practice*. London: Tavistock Press.

Handy, C. (1976) *Understanding Organizations*. London: Penguin.

Handy, C. (1990) *Inside Organizations*. London: BBC Books.

Harber, C. and Davies, L. *School Management and Effectiveness in Developing Countries: The Post-Bureaucratic School*. London: Cassell.

Hargreaves, A. (1991) 'Contrived Conviviality: The Micro-politics of Teacher Collaboration' in J. Blase (ed.) *The Politics of Life in Schools: Power, Conflict and Cooperation*. London: Sage.

Hargreaves, A. *et al.* (2001) *Learning to Change: Teaching Beyond Subjects and Standards*. San Francisco: Jossey-Bass.

Hargreaves, A. and Bascia, N. (eds) (2000) *The Sharp End of Educational Change: Teaching, Leading, and the Realities of Reform*. London: Routledge.

Hargreaves, D. and Hopkins, D. (1993) 'School Effectiveness, School Improvement and Development Planning' in M. Preedy (ed.) *Managing the Effective School*. London: Paul Chapman.

Harris, A., Jamieson, I. and Russ, J. (1996) *School Effectiveness and School Improvement*. London: Pitman.

Herzberg, F. (1966) *Work and the Nature of Man*. New York: Staple Press.

Hofstede, G. (1994) *Uncommon Sense About Organisations: Case Studies and Field Observations*. London: Sage.

Holland, J.H. (2002) *Adaptation in Natural and Artificial Systems: An Introductory Analysis with Application to Biology, Control and Artificial Intelligence*. Boston: MIT Press.

Hollingsworth, S. (1997) *International Action Research: A Casebook for Educational Reform*. London: Falmer.

Hopkins, D. (1993) *A Teacher's Guide to Classroom Research*. Buckingham: Open University Press.

Hopkins, D. (1994) *Schools Make a Difference: Practical Strategies for School Improvement*. London: Resource Base/LWT.

Hopkins, D. (1996) 'Towards a Theory of School Improvement' in Gray, J., Reynolds, D., Fitz-Gibbon, C. and Jesson D. (eds) *Merging Traditions: The Future of Research on School Effectiveness and School Improvement*. London: Cassell.

Hopkins, D. (2001) *School Improvement for Real*. London: Routledge.

Hopkins, D., Ainscow, M. and West, M. (1994) *School Improvement in an era of Change*. New York: Cassell.

Hord, S. (1987) *Evaluating Educational Innovation*. London: Croom Helm.

Huff, A.S. (1990) *Mapping Strategic Thought*. New York: Wiley.

Hustler, D., Cassidy, T. and Cuff, T. (1986) *Action Research in Classrooms and Schools*. London: Allen & Unwin.

ILEA (1984) *Improving Secondary Schools*. London: ILEA.

Jeans, J. (1942) *Physics and Philosophy*. Cambridge: Cambridge University Press.

Jen, E. (ed.) (1990) *Lectures in Complex Systems*. CA: Addison-Wesley.

Jencks, C., Smith, M., Ackland, H., Bane, M., Cohen, D., Gintis, H., Heyns, B. and Micholson, S. (1972) *Inequality: A Reassessment of the Effect of Family and Schooling in America*. New York: Basic Books.

Johnson, S. (2001) *Emergence: The Connected Lives of Ants, Brains, Cities and Software*. New York: Scribner.

Kapra, F. (1996) *The Web of Life*. London: HarperCollins.

Kauffman, S.A. (1993) *Origins of Order: Self-Organization and Selection in Evolution*. Oxford: Oxford University Press.

Kauffman, S.A. (1995) *At Home in the Universe*. New York: Oxford University Press.

Kauffman, S.A. (2000) *Investigations*. Oxford: Oxford University Press.

Kemmis, S. (1993) 'Action Research' in M. Hammersley (ed.) *Educational Research: Current Issues*. London: Open University.

Kemmis, S. and McTaggart, R. (1981) *The Action Research Planner*. Victoria: Deakin University Press.

Klein, M. (1975a) *Envy and Gratitude*. London: Hogarth Press.

Klein, M. (1975b) *The Psycho-analysis of Children*. London: Hogarth Press.

Kuhn, T.S. (1970) *The Structure of Scientific Revolutions*. Chicago: University of Chicago Press.

Kutnick, P. and Stephens, D. (1992) *Qualitative Research in International Education and Development: Its Implications for Teaching, Training and Policy*. Brighton: Centre for International Education, University of Sussex.

Lacey, C. (1977) *The Socialisation of Teachers*. London: Methuen.

Langton, G.C. (1986) 'Studying Artificial Life with Cellular Automata', *Physica* 22D.

Lawrimore, E.W. (2002) *Complexity Made Simple*. Charlotte, NC: Lawrimore.

Lewin, K. (1946) 'Action Research and Minority Problems', *Journal of Social Issues* 2(4): 34–46.

Lewin, K. (1990) 'Beyond Fieldwork: Reflections on Research in Malaysia and Sri Lanka', in Vulliamy, Lewin and Stephens op. cit.

Lewin, K.M. (1993) *Education and Development: The Issues and the Evidence*. London: ODA.

Lewin, K.M. and Stuart, J.S. (1991) (eds) *Education Innovation in Developing Countries: Case Studies of Change-Makers*. London: Macmillan.

Lewin, R. (1992) *Complexity: Life at the Edge of Chaos*. New York: Macmillan.

Lewin, R. (2000) *The Soul at Work: Listen, Respond, Let Go: Embracing Complexity Science for Business Success*. New York: Simon Schuster.

Lincoln, Y.S. and Guba, E. (1985) *Naturalistic Enquiry*. Beverly Hills, CA: Sage.

Little, A. (1988) *Learning from Developing Countries*. London: University of London Institute of Education.

Lorange, P. (2002) *New Vision for Management: Leadership Challenges*. Boston: Pergamon.

Lorenz, E.N. (1967) *Nature and Theory of the General Circulation of the Atmosphere*. Geneva: World Meteorological Organization.

Lorenz, E.N. (1987) *Nature and Theory of the General Circulation of the Atmosphere*. Geneva: World Meteorological Organization.

Lorenz, E.N. (1995) *The Essence of Chaos*. London: UCL Press.

Luhmann, N. (1986) 'The Autopoiesis of Social Systems' in Geyer, F. and van der Zouwen, J. (eds) *Sociocybernetic Paradoxes*. London: Sage.

Luhmann, N. (1990) *Essays on Self-Reference*. New York: Columbia University Press.

Lukes, S. (1974) *Power: A Radical View*. London: Macmillan.

Mac An Ghaill, M. (1992) 'Teachers' Work: Curriculum Restructuring, Culture, Power and Comprehensive Schooling', *British Journal of Sociology of Education* 13(2): 177–199.

MacGilchrist, B., Myers, K. and Reed, J. (1997) *The Intelligent School*. London: PCP.

Maslow, A.H. (1954) *Motivation and Personality*. New York: Harper.

Maslow, A.H. (1987) *Motivation and Personality*. New York: Longman.

Maturana, H. and Varela, F. (1980) *Autopoiesis and Cognition*. Holland: D. Reidel.

Maxcy, S.J. (1991) *Educational Leadership: A Critical Pragmatic Perspective*. New York: Bergin and Garvey.

McGregor, D. (1960) *The Human Side of Enterprise*. New York: McGraw-Hill.

McKernan, J. (1991) *Curriculum Action Research: A Handbook of Methods and Resources for Reflective Practitioners*. London: Kogan Page.

McLennan, B.N. (1973) *Political Opposition and Dissent*. New York: Dunellen.

McTaggart, R. (1991) *Action Research: A Short Modern History*. Geelong: Deakin University Press.

Merry, U. (1995) *Coping with Uncertainty: Insights from the New Sciences of Chaos, Self-Organisation and Complexity*. New York: Praeger.

Miller, E.J. (1983) *Work and Creativity* (occasional papers), London: Tavistock.

Miller, E.J. (1989) *The Leicester Conference* (occasional papers), London: Tavistock.

Miller, E.J. and Rice, A.K. (1967) *Systems of Organisation: The Control of Task and Sentient Boundaries*. London: Tavistock.

Miller, E.J. (2001) *The Systems Dynamics of Organizations: Integrating the Group Relations Approach, Psychoanalytic, and Open Systems Perspectives*. New York: Karnac Press.

Mingers, J. (1994) *Self-Organising Systems: Implications and Applications of Autopoiesis*. New York: Plenum Publishing.

Morgan, G. (1986) *Images of Organization*. London: Sage.

Morgan, G. (1997) *Images of Organization*. Thousand Oaks, CA: Sage.

Morley, L. and Rassool, N. (1999) *School Effectiveness: Fracturing the Discourse*. London: Falmer.

Morrison, K. (2002) *School Leadership and Complexity Theory*. London: RoutledgeFalmer.

Mortimore, P. and MacBeath, J. (eds) (2001) *Improving School Effectiveness*. Milton Keynes: Open University Press.

Mortimore, P. and Sammons, P. (1997) in White, J. and Barber, M. (eds) (1997) *Perspectives on School Effectiveness and School Improvement*. Bedford Way Papers. London: Institute of Education.

Mortimore, P. and Whitty, G. (1997) 'Can School Improvement Overcome the Effects of Disadvantage?' occasional paper. London: Institute of Education.

Mortimore, P., Sammons, P., Stoll, L., Lewis, D. and Ecob, R. (1988) *School Matters: The Junior Years*. Wells, UK: Open Books.

Mullins, J. (2002) 'Raising a Storm', *New Scientist* (July) 175, no. 2353.

Nicolis, G. and Prigogine, I. (1989) *Exploring Complexity*. New York: W. H. Freeman.

Nonaka, I. (1988) 'Creating Organisational Order Out of Chaos: Self-Renewal in Japanese Firms', *California Management Review* 1: 57–73.

Nonaka, I. and Nishiguchi, T. (2001) *Knowledge Emergence: Social, Technical, and Evolutionary Dimensions of Knowledge Creation*. New York: Oxford University Press.

Nonaka, I. and Tacheuchi, H. (1995) *The Knowledge-Creating Company*. Oxford: Oxford University Press.

O'Hanlon, C. (ed.) (1996) *Professional Development through Action Research in Educational Settings*. London: Falmer.

Oldfather, P. and West, J. (1994) 'Qualitative Research as Jazz', *Educational Researcher* 23: 22–26.

Ouston, J., Maughan, B. and Mortimore, P. (1979) 'School Influences' in M. Rutter (ed.) *Developmental Psychiatry* 67–76, London: Heinemann.

Oxfam (2000) *Education Now*. London: Oxfam.

Ozga, J. (1988) *Schoolwork: Approaches to the Labour Process of Teaching*. Milton Keynes: Open University Press.

Parker, D. and Stacey, R. (1994) *Chaos, Management and Economics: The Implications of Non-Linear Thinking*. London: Institute of Economic Affairs.

Peters, E.E. (1991) *Chaos and Order in the Capital Markets: A New View of Cycles, Prices and Market Volatility*. New York: Wiley.

Phillips, H. (2002) 'Not Just a Pretty Face', *New Scientist* (July) 175, no. 2353.

Postle, D. (1989) *The Mind Gymnasium*. London: Macmillan.

Prigogine, I. (1980) *From Being to Becoming*. San Francisco: W. H. Freeman.

Prigogine, I. and Stengers, I. (1984) *Order out of Chaos*. New York: Bantam.

Pring, R. (1996) 'Educating Persons: Putting Education Back into Educational Research', *Scottish Educational Review* 27(2): 101–112.

Rappaport, J. (1984) 'Studies in Empowerment: Introduction to the Issue' in J. Rappaport and R. Mess (eds) *Studies in Empowerment: Steps Towards Understanding an Action*. New York: Haworth Press.

Reynolds, D. (1976) 'The Delinquent School' in P. Woods (ed.) *The Process of Schooling*. London: Routledge & Kegan Paul.

Reynolds, D. and Cuttance, P. (eds) (1992) *School Effectiveness Research, Policy and Practice*. London: Cassell.

Richards, D. (1990) 'Is Strategic Decision Making Chaotic?' *Behavioral Science* 35: 219–232.

Richardson, G.P. (1991) *Feedback Thought in the Social Sciences and Systems Theory*. Philadelphia: University of Philadelphia Press.

Rogers, C. (1967) *On Becoming a Person*. London: Constable.

Roos, J. (1997) 'The Poised Organisation: Navigating Effectively on Knowledge Landscapes', paper presented at the Strategy and Complexity Seminar, London School of Economics, London, 12 February 1997.

Rosenholtz, S. (1989) *Teachers in the Workplace: The Social Organisation of Schools*. London: Longman.

Ruelle, D. (1993) *Chance and Chaos*. London: Penguin.

Rutter, M., Maugham, B., Mortimore, P. and Ouston, J. (1979) *Fifteen Thousand Hours*. London: Open Books.

Sammons, P., Hillman, J. and Mortimore, P. (1995) *Key Characteristics of Effective Schools: A Review of School Effectiveness Research*. Report commissioned by OFSTED, London: Institute of Education and OFSTED: Chapman Publishing.

Sammons, P., Mortimore, P. and Hillman, J. (1996). 'Key Characteristics of Effective Schools: A Response to "Peddling Feel-good Fictions"', *Forum* 38: 88–90.

Sammons, P., Thomas, S. and Mortimore, P. (1997) *Forging Links: Effective Schools and Effective Departments*. London: Paul Chapman.

Scheerens, J. (1992) *Effective Schooling: Research Theory and Practice*. London: Cassell.

Schon, D.A. (1983) *The Reflective Practitioner*. London: Temple Smith.

Schon, D.A. (1987) *Educating the Reflective Practitioner*. London: Jossey-Bass.

Senge, P.M. (1990) *The Fifth Discipline: The Art and Practice of the Learning Organization*. New York: Doubleday.

Senge, P.M. (2000) *Schools that Learn: A Fifth Discipline Fieldbook for Education, Parents, and Everyone Who Cares About Education*. New York: Doubleday.

Slee, R., Weiner, G. and Tomlinson, S. (eds) (1998) *School Effectiveness for Whom? Challenges to the School Effectiveness and School Improvement Movements*. London: Falmer Press.

Stacey, R.D. (1991) *The Chaos Frontier: Creative Strategic Control for Business*. Oxford: Butterworth-Heinemann.

Stacey, R.D. (1993) *Strategic Management and Organizational Dynamics*. London: Pitman.

Stacey, R.D. (1996) *Complexity and Creativity in Organizations*. San Francisco: Berrett-Koehler.

Stacey, R.D. (2001) *Complex Responsive Processes in Organizations: Learning and Knowledge Creation*. New York: Routledge.

Stacey, R.D. (2002) *Strategic Management and Organizational Dynamics: The Challenge of Complexity*. New York: Financial Times.

Sterman, J.D. (1988) 'Deterministic Chaos in Models of Human Behaviour: Methodological Issues and Experimental Results', *System Dynamics Review* 4: 1–2.

Sterman, J.D. (1989) 'Misperceptions of Feedback in Dynamic Decision Making', *Organizational Behavior and Human Decision Processes* 43: 301–335.

Sterman, J.D. (2000) *Business Dynamics: Systems Thinking and Modelling for a Complex World*. Boston: McGraw-Hill.

Stewart, I. (1989) *Does God Play Dice? The Mathematics of Chaos*. Oxford: Blackwell.

Stoll, L. (1996) 'Linking School Effectiveness and School Improvement: Issues and Possibilities' in Gray, J. *et al. Merging Traditions: The Future of Research on School Effectiveness and School Improvement*. London: Cassell.

Stoll, L. and Fink, D. (1996) *Changing Our Schools*. Buckingham: Open University Press.

Stoll, L., Fink, D. and Earl, L. (2002) *It's About Learning (and It's About Time)*. London: RoutledgeFalmer.

Teddlie, C., Kirby, P. and Stringfield, S. (1989) 'Effective Versus Ineffective Schools: Observable Differences in the Classroom', *American Journal of Education* 97: 221–236.

Teubner, G. (ed.) (1988) *Autopoietic Law: A New Approach to Law and Society*. New York: W. de Gruyter.

Trippi, R.H. (ed.) (1995) *Chaos and Non-linear Dynamics in the Financial Markets*. Burr Ridge, Ill.: Irwin.

Troman, G. (2000) 'Teacher Stress in the Low-Trust Society'. *British Journal of Sociology of Education* 21(3): 331–353.

Turquet, P. (1974) 'Leadership, the Individual and the Group' in Gibbard, G.S., Hartman, J.J. and Mann, R.D. (eds) *Analysis of Groups: Contributions to Theory, Research and Practice*. San Francisco: Jossey-Bass.

Ulrich, H. and Probst, G.J.B. (eds) (1984) *Self-organisation and Management of Social Systems: Insights, Promises, Doubts and Questions*. Berlin: Springer-Verlag.

van Velzen, W., Miles, M., Eckholm, M., Hameyer, U. and Robin, D. (1985) *Making School Improvement Work*. Leuven, Belgium: ACCO.

von Krogh, G. and Vicari, S. (1993) *An Autopoiesis Approach to Experimental Strategic Learning, Implementing Strategic Processes: Change, Learning and Co-operation*. Oxford: Blackwell.

von Krogh, G., Nonaka, I. and Nishiguchi, T. (eds) (2000) *Knowledge Creation: A Source of Value*. New York: St. Martin's Press.

Vulliamy, G., Lewin, K. and Stephens, D. (1990) *Doing Educational Research in Developing Countries: Qualitative Strategies*, London: Falmer.

Waldrop, M.M. (1992) *Complexity: The Emerging Science at the Edge of Chaos*. London: Penguin.

Wheatley, M.J. (1992) *Leadership and the New Science: Learning about Organizations from an Orderly Universe*. San Francisco: Berrett-Koehler.

Wheatley, M.J. (1999) *Leadership and the New Science: Discovering Order in a Chaotic World*. San Francisco: Berrett-Koehler.

Wheatley, M.J. (2002) *Turning to One Another: Simple Conversations to Restore Hope to the Future*. San Francisco: Berrett-Koehler.

White, J. and Barber, M. (eds) (1997) 'Perspectives on School Effectiveness and School Improvement', Bedford Way Papers. London: Institute of Education.

Winnicott, D.W. (1971) *Playing and Reality*. London: Tavistock.

Zeleny, M. (ed.) (1980) *Autopoiesis, Dissipative Structures and Spontaneous Social Orders*. Boulder, CO: Westview Press.

Zeleny, M. (1981) *Autopoiesis, A Theory of Living Organizations*. New York: North Holland.

Zimmerman, B.J. (1992) 'The Inherent Drive Towards Chaos' in Lorange, P., Chakravarty, B., van der Ven, A. and Roos, J. (eds) *Implementing Strategic Processes: Change, Learning and Cooperation*. London: Blackwell.

Index